William A. Oberholtzer.

1966.

EUROPE: AN AERIAL CLOSE-UP

EUROPE:

AN AERIAL CLOSE-UP

BY CHARLES E. ROTKIN

BONANZA BOOKS · NEW YORK

This edition published by Bonanza Books,
a division of Crown Publishers, Inc.,
by arrangement with the author.
(A)

CONTENTS

AUTHOR'S NOTE
AND ACKNOWLEDGMENTS

I first started making these pictures in the summer of 1956 when, literally down to earth, I had come to Europe on a series of magazine and newspaper assignments, and thought that photographing Europe from the air might be a fresh way of looking at an old subject. Having made many aerial photographs in the United States, I have been fascinated by the endless patterns that farms and cities present and have long since discovered that the quickest way to know the character of a city is to see it first from the air. From above, you immediately understand which of a city's areas are important, how the principal streets run, and in what direction a city grows or a river flows.

I had long speculated, too, on what the ancient rooftops, crenelated castles and precisely tilled farms of Europe would look like from a few hundred yards in the air, and as soon I knew I was going to Europe, I started culling those magazine files with which I have been associated as well as picture agencies and other sources of photographs, and it was thus that I suddenly realized that there were virtually no aerial pictures available in any of the public sources that I could tap. This piqued my curiosity even further and I began asking the news bureaus of the various foreign government information and tourist offices and received nothing but vagueness as explanation. . . . "It's expensive to charter aircraft in Europe" (true). "There aren't many airplanes available for rental" (truer). "There are many regulations that prohibit this sort of thing" (truest). Yet no one said it was impossible—so I took a long chance, packed my gear and went, first, to England.

There, I had no difficulty. There were no restrictions, other than the usual ones relative to air safety, altitude, and traffic control, and, having made my first set of photographs, I sailed off to Stockholm, saying to myself . . . "Now that wasn't too bad . . ."

In Stockholm I met a member of the Swedish Photographers' Association, who seemed eager to help.

"Do you know where I can rent an airplane to make some photographs?" I asked her.

"From the air?" she asked me, almost incredulously.

"Certainly, why not?"

She then gave me that look of abject pity I have come to know so well, and gently suggested that I had better talk to the Foreign Office.

"Don't you know," thundered the Foreign Office, "that the taking of aerial photographs is prohibited in Sweden except by permission of the Swedish Defense Staff?"

So off I went to the Swedish Defense Staff and, after the initial shock of my request wore off, they finally gave in, on condition that I submit my films to censorship, and that I be accompanied by an observer from the Swedish Air Force to make sure I didn't photograph anything of a military nature.

This was my first brush with censorship and officialdom, and by no means my last. Yet Sweden was mild and reasonable compared to the red tape I have run up against throughout the rest of Europe.

Since my first European trip, I have spent many hours in its museums, galleries, and restaurants, but these pleasant hours are nothing compared to those spent cooling my heels in Air Ministries, Police Prefectures, Customs Offices, and other traps of officialdom.

For example, take Paris. When I first arrived there, my initial visit was not to the Louvre, Eiffel Tower or Tour d'Argent, but to the Ministry of the Interior. On my second day, instead of sitting in a sidewalk café on the Left Bank, I waited for an official of the Police of the Air—just as I have since waited many more times in many other countries.

Yet in retrospect I am not sorry, and am grateful for the experience too, for it gave me an insight into a Europe the average tourist never sees; just as the photographs in this book are a *part* of Europe rarely seen by the tourist.

Of necessity, my bad French became a little better so that I might understand the questions that were being fired at me, and I shudder to think of the confusion that ruled in so many government offices during my frequent attempts to obtain proper permits and clearances. One exchange, I remember well:

"How many motors does your airplane have?"

"None."

"Are you joking?"

"No. I don't own an airplane; I merely want to rent one."

"Ah, if we grant you the permit, how many motors will it have?"

Again, I answered that I didn't know because, until I had the permit, I couldn't find anyone from whom I could rent a plane. And so it went—sometimes frustrating, sometimes funny, but usually ending in a spirit of co-operation that often took the wind out of my sails.

With the exception of England, Denmark, and Switzerland, every country in Europe is snarled in red-tape, censorship, permits, and licenses. Air police patrol the airfields, their alert eyes fixed on all activities involving charter operations. In

France, for instance, in order to take aerial photographs, not only is a special license required from the Ministry of Interior, but also each local Mayor must grant requested permission at least two weeks in advance before flights can be made over his metropolis. With the increase in air traffic, controllers are closing off more and more cities to additional flights and raising minimal altitudes to heights that, if they continue, will make this kind of photography increasingly impossible.

Sometimes, the reason for witholding permits is largely economic, though frequently a permit denial refers, apparently, to military security. In Italy, some years ago, I was told that the bridges over the Tiber were classified! But then a local photographer appeared and offered to sell me aerial photographs of the very bridges that were "military" in nature.

In Vienna, a local operator quadrupled the price on which I had agreed for a charter flight because he was afraid I might use these photographs to make picture postcards in competition with himself.

In another country, which shall remain nameless, my request for clearance was ignored for so long that I left the country, rented a plane in an adjoining one, took my pictures, and then returned to find a message saying that my license would be cleared in another two weeks. . . . This, after having already waited three weeks.

Despite all this, one thing always remained exciting and stimulating. For every bureaucrat and petty official with whom I had to deal, I invariably found two or three others who went out of their way to be helpful. One assistant air secretary became so embarrassed at the inanity of the red-tape that he finally said, "Look, I handle all complaints about aircraft over this city and I am going away for my holidays. The Air Police will simply refer all complaints to me. . . . So please take your pictures without the permit . . . I want our country represented in your book and am embarrassed at the foolishness of those who are making things difficult for you." So I did.

I shall always be grateful to the manager of a local air charter company in Spain who spent two whole weeks shepherding me through the labyrinth of Air Ministries, and then enlisted the cordial co-operation of the Spanish Air Force, a pleasant surprise, even though it did take another two weeks, sweating out the worst weather in Spanish history, before we could finally take our pictures.

I remember too, with much gratitude, the busy Paris doctor, who practically ignored her medical practice to ride herd on the various officials concerned with clearing me, so that I might get through in time.

These are the people to whom I really dedicate this book. They were many and, even though they had their own lives to lead, their own jobs, they nevertheless took time to assist me, make arrangements, track down officials and aircraft, bargain and negotiate with operators and, in general, create an atmosphere of friendliness and warmth that I shall never forget. There were many with whom my contact was fleeting (some I never even saw; the weather forecasters, the traffic controllers, the mechanics who removed an airplane door or installed an extra heating duct). To all of them I say thank you. I hope these results were worth your efforts.

To the people listed below, I am especially grateful, because each in his or her way added something extra that enabled me to complete this project within the limits of time allocated:

Miss Kerstin Bernhard of Stockholm, and Brigadier General Sam Myhrman of the Swedish Defense Staff; Dr. Arlette Fribourg, Paris; Mr. Philippe Waldberg, Mr. Serge Malle and the members of the Paul-Tissander Flying Club of France; M. Piazza and Mme. De Maundit of the Sureté Nationale; Marcel Rivière and Jean Bremont of the newspaper *Le Progrès* (Lyon); and the pilots of their planes; Miss Helen Kahn and Mr. Adrian LaFargue of the Sabena Belgian Airlines; Drs. R. F. Matteisch and Henry Rennau of the Austrian State Tourist Bureau; Miss Lilia Silvestri, Milano; Captain Peter Leewenburgh of the Royal Dutch Air Force; Sr. Guillermo Garcia Diaz of the Politécnica Aérea, S.A., Madrid; Colonel Luis Serrano de Pablo and Captain Joaquin Fernandez Parra of the Spanish Air Force Search and Rescue Squadron; Dr. Estanislão Pan, Director of the Spanish National Tourist Bureau; Mr. A. G. Georgopoulos, IBM Athens; Mr. Costas G. Kyriakos, Director of the Greek Auto Club, Athens; Brigadier General (Ret.) D. F. Scaltsoyannis of the Royal Greek Air Force; Erich and Traudl Lessing, Vienna.

In addition there are those here in New York whose advice and help was invaluable: Mrs. Edith S. Gilmore (historical research and editing); Miss Yvonne Freund; Mr. Brooke Alexander of FORTUNE Magazine; Mrs. Shirley Joel; Mr. Dick Schuler, Mr. Ernie Pile and Miss Sybil Collins of Compo Photo Service.

EUROPE: AN AERIAL CLOSE-UP

ENGLAND

AN AIR VIEW of a great city reveals its individuality; even the rooftops indicate something of the character of its culture. London, old and new, is of particular interest as the heart of a nation with an astonishing history. Before 1500, England was a minor country, relatively remote from the Mediterranean center of European civilization. It had long been entangled in a series of wars for its French possessions, and it was weakened by the domestic Wars of the Roses which led to the establishment of the Tudor monarchs. Their leadership had much to do with England's swift development; by 1700 it was the most powerful nation on earth.

Many lovers of London hope, and say, that the city will never really change, and in fact many of the houses destroyed by the air raids of World War II have been replaced by replicas. But a lover sees at close range; a helicopter view shows that the skyline is altering rapidly. The thirty-story Vickers Building is located almost next to the Tate Gallery with its classical lines, and all over London, towers of aluminum, steel and glass climb high over ancient chimney pots. In The City, the stronghold of the conservative Londoner, and of the Bank of England, the cluster of new buildings around St. Paul's manages to set off the formal beauty of the Christopher Wren masterpiece. But traditionalists are not so easily pleased; they gaze sadly at steamshovels biting into the earth to prepare for still another "outrage" that will rise near the cathedral.

At Hyde Park Corner an underpass is being constructed; the old free-speech arena echoes to the snarl of bulldozers, draglines, and drills; there the human voice is no longer important. Only at night, or on weekends, will you hear that tomorrow, perhaps, the world will end. Near by, the Marble Arch is enshrouded in fencing and building materials, and the jammed traffic threads its way around detours and crossovers.

Along the Thames where once only ships, scows, barges and occasional college shells made quiet progress, the helicopters assert their somehow absurd dignity up and down, back and forth from their landing pad at Battersea. Everywhere are the scars of what some Englishmen mournfully call progress, paying that word what mite of tribute they can. Parking meters stud the city; radar-equipped police provoke thin cries of "unsporting!" parking zones are colored violent pink; and the elevated express highway, or "flyover," inches into the heart of London.

However, much does remain of the serenity of the old city. Along Piccadilly, Regent Street, Bond Street and Haymarket, shining black taxis all built high enough to accommodate a gentleman wearing a top hat, ease in between limousines, lorries, and lethal sports cars. Bowler-hatted men stroll along, each with his tight-rolled umbrella, each sustaining that monument of his own dignity. The newsboys are a contrast: headlines emblazon their placards; they shout splendid Cockney cries.

Or there is Buckingham Palace and the old ceremony of the Changing of the Guard. The tall soldiers in their dramatic bearskins are, in theory, the guardians of the Queen's Residence. In practice, up until recently they needed protection themselves, for ill-bred tourists strained the bonds of decency, in their attempts to make the men smile, scowl, or even blink. Some souvenir hunters went so far as to snip buttons from their uniforms. When a lady tourist was "accidentally" kicked by a Guardsman, the British press, plumping for understatement, expressed only mild reproach.

The English are masters of understatement; they prefer anonymity; they value perseverance, decency, fair play. The Englishman who remarks, with suspicious casualness, that he's done "a little flying" himself, may well be conceding the fact that he was a hero of the Battle of Britain.

Aerial photography, of course, is made difficult by the uncertainties of English climate. All the old jokes on the topic ("We had summer on a Thursday last year") are based on fact, and the omnipresent umbrella and mackintosh represent realistic precaution. The change from clear to cloudy occurs rapidly; the photographer often finds that in the brief time it has taken him to hurry into the air on a sunny morning all photography has become impossible.

English notions of good weather are full of pathos to anyone from happier climes; a "good" day is one that is not out-and-out bad. Weather is a favorite topic of conversation, outranked only by the doings of the royal family and the care of pets. Now and then a truly good day dawns and, hinting of miracles, stays. In fact, there are more of them than some Englishmen will admit, perhaps because—and they are quite right—they take morose pride in their misty climate. It keeps England verdant and clean; in fair weather the countryside, the northern lakes and the coast are clear as plate glass. From the air, the rural lands are green rugs with enchanting toy houses and carved animals. The view becomes grim over the "black country," the soot-blackened houses and factories of the industrial midlands. Even there, however, are scraps of lawn and tiny gardens, for these are essential to most Englishmen's sense of life.

This then, is England today—much changed, little changed—a country that has had untold influence in shaping America and, what is more important, has had a unique hand in shaping the world as we know it today. What we are today, whether good or bad, would have been impossible without England. We may turn to her with the pride of certainty.

LONDON AND THE RIVER THAMES

(Overleaf) The Tower Bridge and the Tower of London dominate the city's threshold, behind which lies the heart and core of the vast metropolis. To the right can be seen the Monument and St. Paul's Cathedral; in the foreground, the St. Katherine Docks.

ians into the Roman armies," wrote Edward Gibbon in his *Decline and Fall of the Roman Empire,* "became every day more universal, more necessary, and more fatal." Rome was captive before she was taken, as the poet Rutilius Namatianus commented early in the fifth century.

By the mid-third century, Imperial Rome was foundering. Dacia was far away and indefensible. The Emperor Aurelian pulled his forces back to the Danube.

Here the army files past the eyes of mounted commanders on the distant hill. The legion's standard, an eagle, is carried by the *aquilifer,* who wears the skin of a wild beast. The *bucinator,* or trumpeter, summons stragglers.

For the next nine centuries Dacia all but disappeared from history. Migrating Goths, Huns, Slavs, Avars, Bulgars, and Germans plundered the land, but Rome's cultural heritage remained strong; the Romanian language, an offspring of Latin, still survives.

LONDINIVM

IN THE THIRD CENTVRY

Three-mile wall protects the London of Roman days

THE FIRST BOMB dropped on London in World War II initiated a new era in the archeology of Roman Londinium. Pits dug by explosives and the bulldozers of postwar rebuilders uncovered coins, lamps, statues, and mosaic floors buried twenty feet beneath a city so congested that archeologists seldom had found an opportunity to excavate it.

Most exciting discovery was the Temple of Mithras, an Asian deity, patron and protector of soldiers. Excavation in the Cripplegate area revealed walls of a fort, or *castra*, enclosing some eleven acres.

Invaded by Julius Caesar (54 B.C.), southern Britain was annexed in A.D. 43 by the Emperor Claudius, and Londinium was founded soon after. But in the year 60 a tribal uprising, led by Queen Boudicca (Boadicea) left the town in ashes and its inhabitants dead. By the early third century, the Romans had built a wall enclosing an earlier fort. Towered gates spanned roads to other towns.

The Romans apparently saw no need of a river wall; none has yet been discovered. Wharves extended directly from warehouses to ships moored in the Thames. Merchant vessels took on cargoes of British slaves, cattle, hunting dogs, silver, iron, and lead. A wooden drawbridge carried traffic into what is now Southwark, on the south bank. Thatched houses flanked mansions. Buildings, baths, and temples created an imposing skyline. The Basilica, with its forum, occupied two blocks (upper right). Merchants, soldiers, and slaves thronged paved streets.

On the western hill (left), now the site of St. Paul's, smoke drifted from kilns and workshops. Fleet River (left) and the Walbrook (left, center) flowed above ground where they now run in sewers.

As Roman power crumbled in the western provinces, the emperors withdrew troops. Londinium sank into obscurity.

New Data From Noted Authorities

To create this map, the National Geographic Society sent staff artist Robert W. Nicholson to London to visit museums, take photographs, and consult archeologists and historians. He found sites of wall, fort, Basilica, and Temple of Mithras firmly established. Road alignments and Roman coins taken from the Thames located the drawbridge. In the case of other features, notably the imposing temple dominating the center of the city, exact sites are unknown, and their locations on the map reflect the informed assumptions of leading authorities.

The Society could not have prepared the map without the guidance of Prof. W. F. Grimes, Director of the Institute of Archeology at London University and Honorary Director of Excavations for the Roman and Mediaeval London Excavation Council; Norman Cook, Keeper of the Guildhall Museum; and Ralph Merrifield, an assistant keeper at the Museum. From their great knowledge, these men gave the Society material never before correlated and published.

KEY TO PAINTING

FLEET RIVER
NEWGATE
ST. PAUL'S CATHEDRAL
KILNS
QUARRIES
WALBROOK
SOUTHWARK
CANNON STREET BRIDGE
TEMPLE OF MITHRAS
BATH
TEMPLE
ALDERSGATE
FORT
GUILDHALL
CANNON STREET STATION
MANSION HOUSE
MERCHANT VESSEL
LONDON BRIDGE
CRIPPLEGATE
CITY WALL
LARGE VILLA
LARGE VILLA
TEMPLES
TEMPLE
BASILICA AND FORUM
BROAD STREET STATION
LIVERPOOL STREET STATION
RIVER THAMES
PRESENT SHORELINE
THE MONUMENT (COMMEMORATING THE GREAT FIRE, 1666)
BATH
LLOYD'S
GRANARY
BILLINGSGATE MARKET
PLANTATION HOUSE
BATH
CEMETERY
BISHOPSGATE
FISHING CRAFT

DIAGRAM BY S. STEFANOFF © N.G.S.

Key shows important features of Londinium in red and orients them with landmarks of today's city.

Chained, a runaway tenant pleads with his Roman lord

KNEELING in the columned courtyard of his master's villa, a wretched tenant farmer pours out his anguish: Life was too hard... he could not meet the burdens imposed upon him... despair seized him... he had tried to escape.... Forgive, forgive.

The wealthy landlord and his son (right) show only hardhearted disdain. Though legally free, this man was bound by law to work their estate. The Emperor Constantine's law, dated October, 332, was emphatic: "Tenant farmers who meditate flight are to be put in chains and reduced to... servitude."

The tragedy of this scene was generations in the making. During Rome's early days the small freeholder, cultivating his own acres and fighting when necessary, had been the backbone of the Republic. But as Rome embarked on a career of conquest, soldiering became a profession, and many farmers abandoned the plow to seek their fortunes in war.

Foreign grain flooded the Italian market; small farmers could not compete. Slaves replaced free labor, and gold flowed only into the pockets of rich landowners. Debt drove thousands into the cities. In Rome they joined the mob that rulers placated with bread and circuses. Wealthy men built up vast estates, worked by *coloni*, or tenants.

By the third century the Pax Romana—the Roman Peace—had vanished; improved leadership barely restored it in the fourth. War and famine threatened on every side. Cities decayed, commerce stagnated, and population declined. Landed aristocrats raised what they needed on their own estates. Much land passed out of cultivation. There was no security for the poor.

Emperor Valentinian III thus describes the grim winter of 450-451: "It is well known that very recently the most terrible famine wasted a province..."

Restored Villa Echoes the Delights of Pompeii

Luxury-loving Romans built handsome homes in the mountain-flanked city. Good times abruptly turned into tragedy in the year 79, when Mount Vesuvius erupted.

The death-dealing blanket of ash and cinders preserved a remarkable record of life in ancient times. Archeologists have unearthed villas complete even to statues and paintings. (See NATIONAL GEOGRAPHIC, November, 1961.)

As restored, House of the Vettii has fountains, a garden, and murals that glow with color or applied almost 2,000 years ago. Villa opposite resembles this Pompeii mansion.

KODACHROME BY MICHAEL MARLOW © NATIONAL GEOGRAPHIC SOCIETY

HOUSES OF PARLIAMENT

The Union Jack, flying over the 336-foot Victoria Tower, indicates that the third oldest parliament in the world is in session. Long before the Norman Conquest, King Canute occupied a palace on this site. The first Westminster Palace was built in 1097; Richard II ordered it rebuilt in 1394, when Westminster Hall, with its magnificent hammer-head roof, was added. The huge building was used in those days as both a Royal Residence and a Parliament building. In 1834 it was partly destroyed by fire, and when rebuilt, the Central Tower and Clock Tower were added, as well as new chambers for the House of Commons. The new House of Commons was again badly damaged during the bombings of 1941.

To the left of Parliament are Westminster Abbey and St. Margaret's Church, with the statues of great men ringing Parliament Square. One American is among them: Abraham Lincoln.

Behind Parliament, other government offices stretch up Parliament Street toward Whitehall and Trafalgar Square. At the left is a group of buildings housing the Treasury and Foreign Office, and at the right is New Scotland Yard and Downing Street where, at Number 10, the Prime Minister resides.

BIG BEN

(Left) London's most famous landmark, Big Ben, is not named for the ornate four-sided clock in the 316-foot tower, as most visitors think, but for the twenty-six-ton bell which has been clanging hourly ever since Sir Benjamin Hall, the first Works Commissioner, installed it in 1858.

THE DOME OF ST. PAUL'S

(Above) Inspiring for tourists and Londoners are the dome and galleries of St. Paul's Cathedral. The Whispering Gallery magnifies the faintest sound; the Stone and Golden Galleries offer a much advertised view of the City; from the tiny Ball Room under the roof the cathedral floor is visible 300 spinning feet below.

ST. PAUL'S CATHEDRAL

Ludgate Hill, overlooking the Thames, has been the site of three known churches of St. Paul; even before the first one was erected in the 7th century, legend holds that a Christian church stood on this rise, later destroyed by the Romans. The first Cathedral of St. Paul was burned in 1087. A second was started and took more than a hundred years to build—John Donne was its Dean in the 17th century—only to fall into disrepair and eventually go down in the Fire of 1666.

Christopher Wren, at the time a young architect, had already received a commission from Charles II to plan the repair and remodeling of the edifice, but the razing by fire gave him an opportunity to start from the ground up. Heavily influenced by the architecture of St. Peter's in Rome, he broke away (against much conservative opposition) from English Gothic. Typically of the way genius is treated, he was not allowed to do quite as he liked, but Charles II did grant him sufficient authority to carry out his basic ideas. The new Cathedral was begun in 1675 and finished forty-five years later. Wren was about eighty at the time, and when he died in 1723 he was buried in his masterpiece under his own inscription, *"Lector, si monumentum requiris, circumspice."* (Reader, if you seek my monument, look about you.)

At one time the 366-foot-high cross was the tallest structure in London, but now office buildings rising on all sides, and farther up the Thames, are beginning to dwarf it. Luckily it survived the blitz, though buildings all around were demolished. Thousands of Britons took refuge in its vast halls during air raids and many of them are certain that it was not by chance that St. Paul's was spared.

BUCKINGHAM PALACE

(Above) The site of Buckingham Palace, the London residence of Queen Elizabeth II and the Duke of Edinburgh, was bought and built upon in 1703 by the Duke of Buckingham, and sold to George III in 1762. It was rebuilt in 1825 by John (Beau) Nash, and under Queen Victoria became the royal residence in London. In the upper left is the Green Park; in front of the palace stands the monument to Victoria. The Green Park is separated from Hyde Park by Piccadilly (row of buildings at top of photo). The Wellington Memorial and Hyde Park Corner are at the extreme upper left. Soapbox orators use an area of Hyde Park near the Marble Arch. *(Right)* The bare flagpole on top of the palace indicates that the Queen is not in residence, but the Changing of the Guard takes place every morning at eleven (except that it is shifted to St. James's Palace if the Queen is not in London).

The Mall stretches up from Buckingham to the Admiralty Arch adjacent to Trafalgar Square. In the group of buildings in the left foreground are Lancaster House, Clarence House and St. James's Palace. St. James's was the Royal Residence until the time of Victoria. Upper left are St. James's Square and Pall Mall. The latter terminates at Haymarket, near Trafalgar Square.

TOWER BRIDGE AND THE TOWER OF LONDON

Of London's many landmarks none is so often confused with another as is Tower Bridge. For generations, school children have sung "London Bridge is falling down," and have grown up with the fixed impression that Tower Bridge is the bridge of the song. (The actual London Bridge is farther up-river.) Nor is this curious-looking structure medieval, as some people assume; it was completed in 1894. Two architects designed it so that the river traffic could pass under its twenty-nine-foot clearance, and also to accommodate the tallest-masted vessels when its thousand-ton lifting bascules are raised.

Many aspects of medieval political life in England are symbolized, authentically and grimly, by the Tower of London, or, officially, Her Majesty's Royal Fortress and Palace of the Tower of London. In the center is the White Tower, begun by William the Conqueror and finished by his son Rufus, who also added the hexagonal wall and the thirteen towers that surround the central keep. Nearest the river is Bloody Tower. This, and Wakefield Tower, were stopping-off places on the way to the headsman's block on Tower Hill. Also you will see, hopping grotesquely about the towers, the Royal Ravens who, ominously, rarely croak and caw, and whose suspicious little eyes, briefly suggesting the nearby Crown Jewels, fix you malevolently. Indeed, like the Crown Jewels, these

huge birds, with their silent sidewise hop, can be unnerving: each of them is as real as a severed head.

Among those who passed through Traitor's Gate to their doom were two of the wives of Henry VIII, Anne Boleyn and Catherine Howard; also the Duke of York, his brother Edward V, and Sir Walter Raleigh. Sir Walter, however, managed to survive for thirteen "pleasant" years in the Tower with his family, writing his *History of the World* and receiving friends, including Prince Henry. Released in 1616 for a last expedition, which failed, he was beheaded two years later at the demand of the Spanish ambassador.

The Tower has not been used as a place of execution since 1747, and is now essentially a museum of antiquities and a barracks and residence for some 600-800 people, chiefly troops and officers who carry out the ancient ceremonies. Every night a ritual known as the Ceremony of the Keys takes place from 9:53 to exactly 10:00, when the locking of the gates is supposed to be completed. Since the Crown Jewels of England are kept in the Tower, the security precautions are more than mere ritual. The Chief Warder, carrying a lantern, makes the rounds every night with a detail of guards, and the prescribed words, with a Shakespearian ring about them, are exchanged on the night air: "Halt . . . who goes there? . . . Keys . . . Whose keys? . . . Queen Elizabeth's keys. . . . Advance Queen Elizabeth's keys . . . All's well . . . God preserve Queen Elizabeth . . . Amen."

WESTMINSTER ABBEY

No one really knows how far back into history Westminster Abbey goes or the churches which preceded it. An early monastery destroyed by the Danes was extensively rebuilt in the 11th century by Edward the Confessor, the first monarch to be buried there. His successor, William the Conqueror, was crowned in the Abbey, which for the next seven hundred years was the setting for all British coronations and royal burials. The last king to be buried there was George II in 1760.

The Abbey is also the final resting-place for many commoners, some great, some near great, and some downright humble—the Abbey plumber, a prizefighter, an actress. And many of those who through the centuries have contributed to the stream of English cultural life—literary, musical or scientific—have been accorded a grave in the Abbey or a commemorative plaque or monument. Chaucer, Spenser and Tennyson are interred there; so are Dryden, Purcell, Darwin and Newton. Ben Jonson is there too, buried standing erect, according to his last instructions. O rare Ben Jonson.

ST. MARGARET'S

(*Above*) To the left of the Abbey is a beautiful little church, St. Margaret's, which is often overlooked by visitors. It was built in 1523 and its East Window is considered to be the loveliest stained-glass window in England. Sir Walter Raleigh was buried here after his execution in 1618.

25

COURTS OF JUSTICE

The Royal Courts of Justice occupy this handsome neo-Gothic structure on the edge of Fleet Street, which is better known for its newspaper offices and its traditional memories of Dr. Johnson and Oliver Goldsmith. Indeed, the Old Cheshire Cheese, that inn where Johnson held forth among his entourage, still stands in the Wine Office Court off Fleet Street and still serves drinks to astonishing crowds of journalists. It is worth your while, once, to elbow your way into this crush, to lift a sentimental glass.

To the lower left is St. Clement Dane's Church and, in the background, the Royal College of Surgeons.

26

THE MONUMENT

Christopher Wren designed this 202-foot tower in commemoration
of the Great Fire which burned for five days in 1666 and virtually
leveled London. For those willing to pay any physical price for a
good guidebook view, the monument is the place to go. An inside
stairway of 345 steps affords, if strength and virtue hold out, a
panorama of London's East End.

We pop in on London 44 times a week.

BOOKS >>>

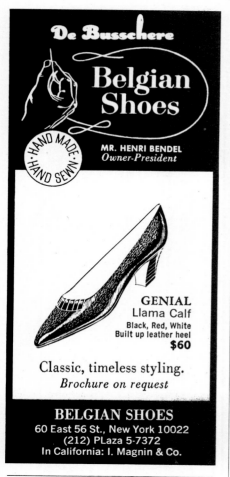

ture, things were best left as they were.

This may sound as if the book were a mere sociological survey. It is far from that. There are enthralling accounts of trips deep into the Sahara, of lost cities, of harems, of the unfortunate passion of a shiek for a German school teacher—all this written with the wry zest of the best kind of traveling American: a woman, educated, humorous, who keeps her eyes open.

It is exactly this sense of vivid personality that is the chief lack of **Three Tickets to Timbuktu** by Halla Linker (Putnam). Halla and David Linker are well known professional travelers, whose world-ranging trips have been made into a popular television series. But for all their energy, courage and determination, people like the Linkers (at least as they portray themselves here) remain basically parochial because they apply their own rather conventional standards to everything they see; what is more, they feed this predigested world to millions lacking a fraction of their own resourcefulness. This is not to say the book isn't lively and readable; there's just nothing to chew on.

Eighteen months ago Luigi Barzini scored a considerable success with a book on the Italians. Nirad Chaudhuri deserves a similar success for his study of the people of India, **The Continent of Circe** (Oxford); he probably won't get it, however, partly because his subject does not appeal to the popular imagination as much as Signor Barzini's and partly because his style lacks the aphoristic sparkle of "The Italians." Nevertheless, Mr. Chaudhuri's is an extraordinary achievement. Unlike many educated Indians, he received his schooling entirely in his native land. This shows as a drawback in the occasional stiffness or angularity of the

du private and public behavior on the supposition that they have a normal personality."

Open his book almost anywhere and you will find revealing light thrown on the Indian character, so often the despair of other peoples. Hindus suffer, he says, from the enormous tension of contrary pulls: they are basically militaristic and jingoistic, but have to live up to a world image as nonviolent neutralists; they suffer from bottomless *accidie,* which inspires them to mockery of effort, but can become savagely violent and abusive in quarrel; their sex life, after centuries of effort to rejuvenate flagging powers in line with obsessional dedication (Mr. Chaudhuri is particularly interesting on the psychology of the Oriental love manuals now flooding the West), is torpid and hysterical by turn, and their religious observance has the quality of sentimental fetishism. All this is strong stuff, but it does seem to clarify many previously puzzling contradictions in the Indian personality; and at least India can ruefully congratulate herself on having produced so independent-minded and fearless an interpreter.

I can't imagine a better book to take with you anywhere in the Caribbean than **From the Green Antilles** (Macmillan). Barbara Howes' selection of imaginative prose and verse by Antilleans of various cultures is that most invaluable of all guidebooks: a guide to the amenities and the history of the human heart.

Considering the handicaps faced by the writer in the islands—a less than first class educational system, a limited audience, the difficulty of getting published except at a great distance from his source material—the work collected here is of astonishingly high quality. Those writers who are fortunate

TRAFALGAR SQUARE AND NELSON'S MONUMENT

The 185-foot shaft protected by four bronze lions and flanked by plumed fountains is a tribute to Lord Nelson's victory at Trafalgar in 1805 against a French-Spanish fleet. It was this victory that established Britain's supremacy at sea and awakened Napoleon from his dream of the conquest of England.

On the left is Admiralty Arch, gateway to Whitehall and the route of most state processions from Westminster. In the upper right is St. Martin in the Fields Church, a landmark since 1726. Behind the main square is the National Gallery of Art, containing in addition to the collection of British masters (Gainsborough, Reynolds, Hogarth) an oustanding group of Holbeins and Van Dycks.

In front of the gallery, weather permitting, artists crayon their pictures on the sidewalk. Years ago, one of them, a destitute French painter, called himself Maurice Vlaminck. The square itself is a frequent gathering place for political protests. But usually, and in all innocence, the Square is inhabited by nothing more than swarms of pigeons and starlings whose cooing and chirping, every evening, drown the roar of traffic as they settle for the night along surrounding ledges and rooftops.

29

WHITEHALL—REGENT STREET

(Above) The War Office and St. James's Park. The Mall (upper right) leads to Buckingham Palace across the park. In the foreground: Charing Cross Station and a wedge of the Embankment. (Below) Admiralty Arch commands the gateway to Whitehall, with the Admiralty Building and the Horse Guards Barracks on its left. On the other side of the Mall, the Duke of York Monument stands, with Kiplingesque certainty of Empire, at the foot of Lower Regent Street. (Right) Regent Street with its fine shops curves up to Piccadilly Circus. Lower Regent Street comes down from the upper right.

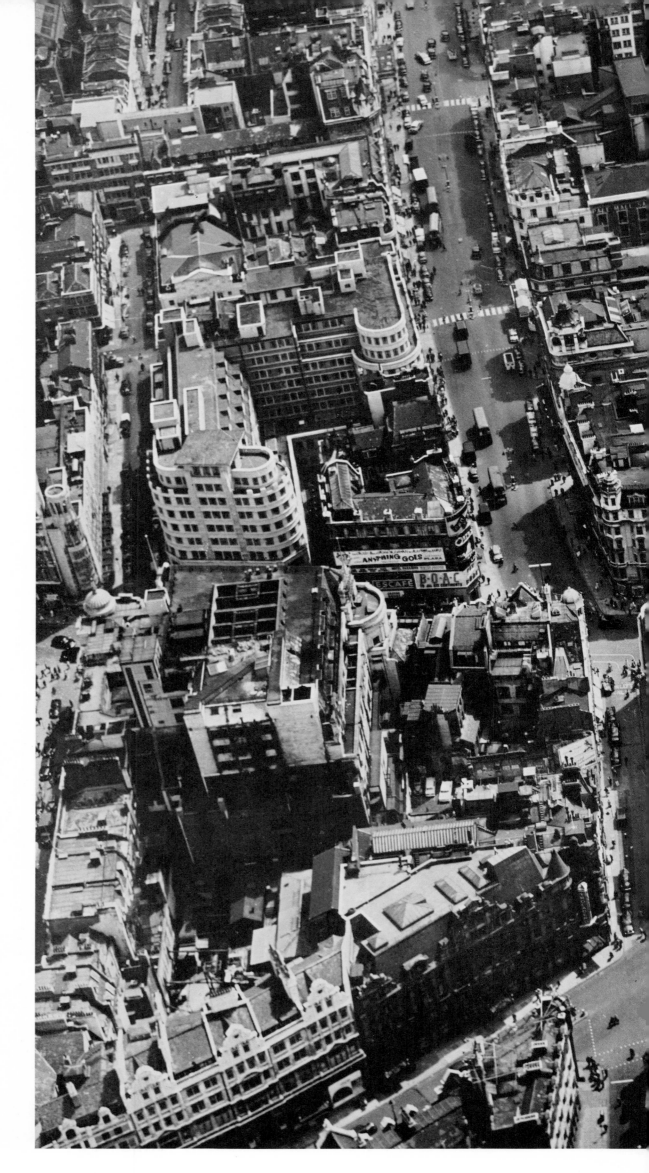

PICCADILLY CIRCUS

Piccadilly Circus is London's Times Square, and Londoners rightly hold that sooner or later everyone in the world can be met there.

This gay center is a good, if confusing, place in which to celebrate New Year's Eve or, no less obviously, to enjoy a late pint after the cinema or the theater. If you are young, exuberant, enjoy a climb, and are homeless, you can express yourself by a casual scaling of the Statue of Eros. Your lodging for the night, instantaneously realized, will be jail.

From this "hub of the universe," many well-known streets radiate. Upper left is Haymarket, running into Coventry Street (which if followed to the left goes to Leicester Square). The triangular building to the left of Eros is a movie house, the London Pavilion, and across the Circus is the Criterion Theater. Shaftsbury Avenue with its theaters (Lyric, Globe, Apollo and others) extends into the lower left. Regent Street and Lower Regent Street are on the right.

ST. MARTIN IN THE FIELDS

(Left) This charming early 18th-century church stands at the edge of Trafalgar Square. Charing Cross Road, with its multitude of bookstores, begins here and curves around the National Gallery.

ST. MARY'S-LE-STRAND

(Below) In the fan-shaped cluster of buildings arching around Aldwych is India House (directly behind the tiny St. Mary's-le-Strand Church) and Australia House at the right edge of the arc. Part of King's College is in the lower left. Behind the main group of buildings and angling off to the left is Drury Lane, part of London's theater center, along with the Strand and Haymarket.

THE TATE GALLERY

The Tate Gallery, on the Thames south of Chelsea above Lambeth Bridge, is one of England's great museums, and houses not only a fine collection of British masters (Turner, Blake, Reynolds) but also many French Impressionists and moderns.

HAMPTON COURT PALACE

(Below) This splendid Tudor palace about ten miles up the Thames from London was begun in 1514 by Cardinal Wolsey, and was finished in 1520. According to legend, it was subsequently "presented" to Henry VIII in 1526 as a gift, though the facts seem to indicate that Wolsey had fallen into disfavor with Henry because of his aspirations to the papacy and was forced into making it a peace offering.

Henry converted it into a royal residence, and for a brief period, at least, every one of his six wives lived there.

Part of the building is now divided into flats for former government officials and deserving pensioners, but much of it is open to the public. Its famous gardens include a maze, into which (surely) some, if not all, of Henry's wives wandered and backtracked, and a greenhouse which protects a grape vine planted almost two hundred years ago, whose grapes are sold off each year for charity. The elaborate parterre, designed by French artists of the School of Le-Notre, is now greatly diminished, but there is a charming sunk garden in Tudor style, spectacularly floral in summer, and the Great Water, a half-mile long.

THE THAMES

(Right) From its headwaters one hundred miles west of London, past Oxford and Windsor and down to London itself before it empties into the North Sea near Gravesend, the Thames is England's historic waterway. It was a public highway long before there were passable roads, and the river-men had a sound reputation for being the roughest, toughest boatmen in Europe. From London to the sea, its roadstead teems with passenger ships, freighters, tugs and barges; its banks are lined with warehouses, shipyards and chandlers. West of London, its activity is chiefly limited to small boats, a few scows, and excursion steamers jammed with tourists.

The Royal Regatta at Henley-on-Thames attracts racing enthusiasts from all over the world, and farther up the river at Oxford the college shells skim those classic waves whenever the weather is fine, and even, as is more frequently the case, when it is not.

WINDSOR CASTLE

One of the great castles of the world, Windsor lies twenty-two miles upstream from London. The origins of this immense structure go back to William the Conqueror, who established a hunting lodge there. However, the most extensive construction was not started until the reign of Henry III, who built the Round Tower (center of compound) in 1272. Almost every subsequent ruler has added something. St. George's Chapel *(lower left)* was begun by Edward IV in 1477 and finished in 1516 by Henry VII.

A giant preserve of almost 2000 acres, Great Windsor Park lies to the south of the Castle. Many wild deer still roam there, and currently a series of unusually fine gardens are being planted. Castle and Park are open to the public, and crowds of visitors come to see its antiquities and to walk under some of the oldest trees in England. In the Castle's extensive galleries hangs a collection of Gobelin tapestries, and paintings by Rubens, Holbein and Van Dyck.

You might, while you are in the vicinity, drop in upon Eton, England's most famous "public" school, just across the river.

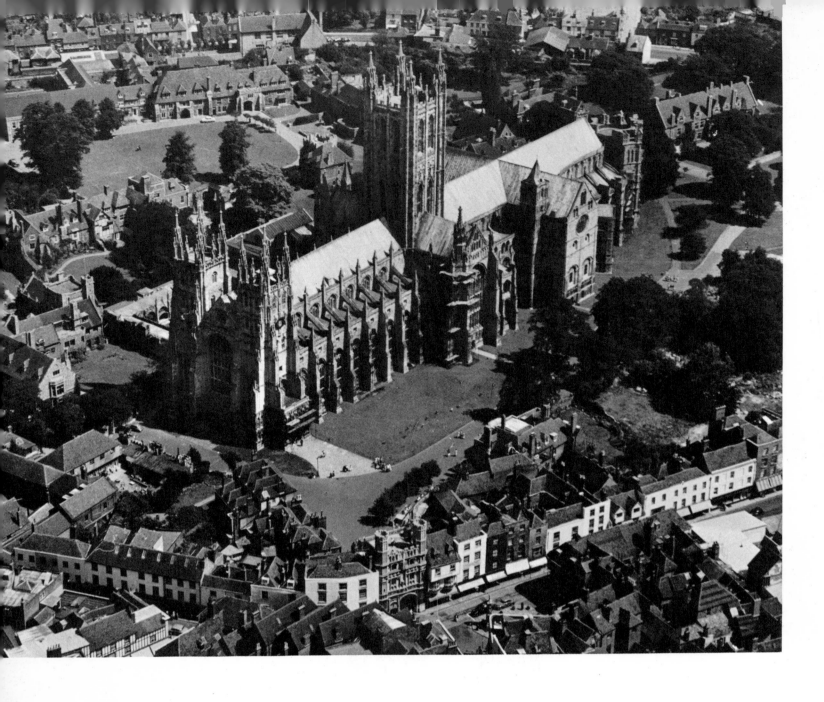

CANTERBURY

(Above) This Cathedral, standing since 1070, is the spiritual heart of England. St. Augustine, founder of English Christianity and first Archbishop of Canterbury, built a church here in the 6th century.

In the northwest transept, Thomas à Becket was slain by order of his former friend and patron, the 12th-century monarch Henry II. Henry appointed Thomas to the Archbishopric under the assumption that his old friend would support his attempts to curb the powers of the ecclesiastical courts, then discovered his error too late and, after lengthy quarrels with Becket, ordered his murder—or so it was assumed by outraged Christendom. Modern treatments of this powerful theme have been written by dramatists in England (Eliot's *Murder in the Cathedral*) and in France (Anouilh's *Becket*) in recent years.

OXFORD

The most famous university town in the world, Oxford is also a city unique for its riches of architecture and collections of many kinds known largely only to specialists. The picture above looks eastward over Christ Church College, known to Oxonians as The House, with its adjoining 12th-century chapel, which is also the Cathedral of Oxford. The great quadrangle, originally designed for a cloister, is dominated by Tom Tower. Old Tom, the bell, strikes 101 times each night at nine, a tradition from the days when one stroke of the bell recalled each of the 101 undergraduates to college before the gates closed. Beyond the trees is the little quad of Corpus Christi College, and immediately north of it Oriel, recognizable by the pointed windows of its early 17th-century dining hall. The large chapel is that of Merton, the most ancient college of all. The tower of Magdalen rises in the distance. From Magdalen

the High Street curves back to the center of town. North of it are the two Georgian quads of Queen's College; beyond these the buildings of 14th-century New College, with its gardens enhanced by the ancient crenelated city wall.

The view on the opposite page, looking southeast toward Magdalen, shows "the Broad," running parallel to "the High": in the left foreground Balliol; next the garden of Trinity, and opposite, farther on, the curved façade of the Sheldonian Theatre, guarded by its weatherbeaten stone emperors, which feature in Max Beerbohm's *Zuleika Dobson*. Above it is the Bodleian Library, and adjoining, the dome of its reading room, the Radcliffe Camera. To the left of that are the twin towers (one under scaffolding) of All Souls College, which has no undergraduates but of which a fellowship is one of the greatest academic honors in the world. T. E. Lawrence was a Fellow of All Souls; Christopher Wren was another.

SURREY—KENT

(Above) Row houses in a residential suburb near Croyden in Surrey County. Despite a high-density population, English householders have always managed to preserve their front and backyard garden patches, and the county itself is often referred to as England's kitchen garden.

(Below) Dover Castle, over the chalk cliffs, has been a fortress since Norman times. The cliffs are honeycombed with tunnels and powder magazines. During World War II, Nazi long-range artillery based in France twenty miles across the Channel pounded the fort and the city continuously; and the Port of Dover, one of the ancient Cinque Ports, served as a springboard for the Allied invasion of Normandy. The lighthouse on the cliff, built by the Romans 2000 years ago is probably the oldest building in England today. Below on the beaches are seaside hotels.

KENT

Oast houses on a hop farm in Kent. If it were not for these odd-looking structures with their little white ventilators like nuns' caps, England's countless pubs would have long since called "time!", for the hops used in brewing English beer are dried and stored here.

SCOTLAND

SCOTLAND is part of Great Britain—officially. The Union of the Crowns in 1603 placed James VI of Scotland, son of Mary Stuart, on the English throne as James I; the Act of Union in 1707 transformed the English Parliament into a British Parliament by the inclusion of Scottish lords and commoners. But then, many centuries of Scotland's existence as an independent Kingdom are still remembered. Even today, some Scots still consider their country as "occupied," and are quick to point out Scottish-British differences of speech, dress and customs. Scottish motorists taking their cars to the continent tend to use international identity tags with the word "Ecosse" under the standard GB symbol; this prevents their being mistaken for English. Nor is the use of the French word for Scotland accidental. Scottish relations with England through the centuries were stormy; Scotland often relied on alliance with France; and the cultural ties have lingered long.

Scottish affection for France was not sufficient, however, to make less bitter the lot, in her own country, of the young Mary Stuart, daughter of a Scottish king and a French mother, widow of a king of France, rightful Queen of Scotland and—unluckily for her—heiress presumptive to the throne of England after the childless Elizabeth. Her melodramatic career included marriage to Bothwell, the man suspected of murdering her second husband, Darnley, whose attempted coup d'état had caused Mary to flee, briefly, from Edinburgh. As the Catholic Queen of a country chiefly Presbyterian, she was opposed by the famous divine, John Knox, and eventually was imprisoned by the Scottish nobles. She then abdicated and made the mistake of escaping to England, which was in the thick of those religious difficulties that followed Henry VIII's break with Rome. As Catholic heiress to the throne, Mary was a dangerous person, a rallying point for English Catholicism. Plotting and plotted against, she was imprisoned, and met her death on the scaffold in 1587, to survive as a romantic heroine.

If Mary's period is still vividly real to the Scottish imagination and memory, so too are the earlier times and events symbolized by the clans and their tartans. Stone-age Picts, Celts from Ireland, tribes from the European mainland settled Scotland and formed the close-knit family group which in time became the Scottish clans. Not many direct descendants of these original clans are left; few people can readily identify all available tartans.

EDINBURGH CASTLE

The battlements and turrets of Edinburgh Castle rise high from Castle Rock, a bluff called by Stevenson one of the most "satisfactory crags in nature." The site has been fortified since the 5th century, overlooking "Auld Reekie." Royalty lived in the castle from the 11th century. In the foreground is the Half Moon Battery, behind it the Argyll Battery and finally St. Margaret's Chapel and parts of the original castle. On the left is the Palace containing the Great Hall and King's Lodging, as well as the barracks and hospital. Below the castle are St. Cuthbert's and St. John's.

Queensferry Street (center) runs northwest toward the Firth of Forth. Princes Street Gardens are on the right, and Johnston Terrace curves down from the left towards the Royal Mile.

THE ROYAL MILE

The small puff of smoke hovering over the castle indicates that the one-o'clock gun has been fired from Halfmoon Battery which stands over the Castle's entry. At the lower left is Tolbooth St. John's Church. The road from the castle to Holyrood Palace *(right)*, called the Royal Mile, was the route Mary Stuart followed when she re-entered Edinburgh with Bothwell.

SCOTT MONUMENT

At the east end of Princes Street stands the 200-foot memorial to Sir Walter Scott, who died in 1832. In the central archway is a statue of Sir Walter, with his dog, Maida. A stairway to the top of the monument is open to the public.

PRINCES STREET

This elegant thoroughfare, the main shopping avenue of Edinburgh, starts on its west end at Princes Street Station and follows the Gardens, past the Royal Scottish Academy and the Scott Monument to its easterly end at Waterloo Place. To the right of the Monument is Waverley Station, and behind it the North British Hotel.

HOLYROOD PALACE

(Below) The Palace of Holyrood, at the easterly end of the Royal Mile, suffered extensive damage throughout the centuries from English soldiers and Protestant mobs. However, the apartments occupied by Mary Stuart for six years after her return to Edinburgh escaped destruction and remain much as they were almost four hundred years ago. Mary's secretary, the young musician David Rizzio, was murdered here.

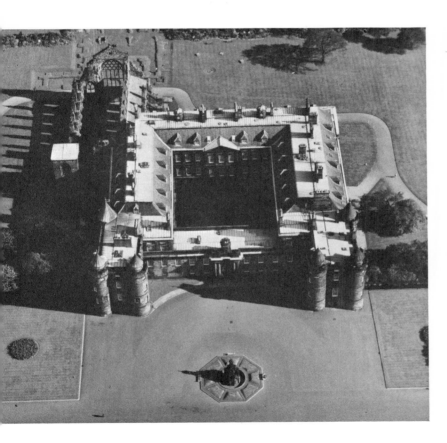

STIRLING CASTLE

(*Above*) Seventy miles northwest of Edinburgh, where the River Forth comes down from the Highlands, ancient Stirling Castle, gray and foreboding, sits high on its precipice. This old fort has been a royal residence since the 10th century, and dominates those plains on which many bloody battles were fought between English and Scots. Robert Bruce defeated Edward II here at the battle of Bannockburn in 1314, thereby reëstablishing Scottish independence after a brief subjection.

Stirling had been taken by the British in 1296 and recaptured by Sir William Wallace in the Battle of Stirling Bridge the following year. It was again retaken by the troops of Edward I, the last castle to hold out against him. When it surrendered, its garrison was reduced to less than 150 men. It is now the headquarters for the Argyle and Sutherland Highlanders, one of the most famous British Regiments.

THE WALLACE MEMORIAL

(*Upper right*) On the River Forth's opposite bank this monument to Sir William Wallace stands in memory of his victory at Stirling Bridge, when he led his men from Dundee to recapture Stirling Castle. Wallace also defeated the English at Falkirk in 1298 but, at last, fell into their hands. After his execution his head was exposed on a pike on London Bridge.

LINLITHGOW PALACE

(Right) Thirteen miles from Edinburgh, on the edge of Linlithgow Loch, this ancient ruin was the birthplace of Mary Stuart in 1542. It was also the site of the murder of her half-brother the Earl of Moray who, with the support of John Knox, had attempted to seize the throne in order to make Protestantism secure.

THE KINGDOM OF FIFE

The lovely rich lands and handsome villages across the River Forth are in Fife, a self-styled "kingdom" steeped in Scottish history. This little village is just a few miles to the east of Dunfermline, whose ruined abbey was originally built by King David as a memorial to his mother Saint Margaret, and which once protected the bones of Robert Bruce. The farmlands below raise those grains used to make Scotch whiskey and to feed the land's Angus cattle.

FIRTH OF FORTH BRIDGE

(Right) The bridge at the right is the famous Firth of Forth Bridge at Queensferry just northwest of Edinburgh. It extends for a mile and three quarters across the estuary. Completed in 1890, it has a clearance of 150 feet over high water, and its huge cantilever trusses rear to 361 feet. Built as a railway bridge, it is considered one of the world's great engineering feats. Foot and automobile passengers have a harder but more picturesque time of it: they are carried by the little ferry at the right. But a new suspension bridge, under construction a little farther on, will be open to traffic in 1963, and the little ferry will no longer make its daily crossings.

HOLLAND

Windmills still pump water from the
polder behind the dikes near Rotterdam.

HOLLAND

JUST as the word "English" evokes certain real stereotypes, so does the word "Dutch." The "Dutch treat," for example, is exactly that: the Dutch business man who invites someone to join him for lunch does not expect to pay your check as well as his own. The legend which all children associate with Holland, of the little boy with his finger in the dike, however mythical, is essentially relevant; and every new visitor is reminded of it, often dramatically. For Holland's life and history is bounded by the North Sea. A large part of the nation is below sea level. In their need to find room for crops, housing and industry, the Dutch have reclaimed space from swamps and from the bottom of the sea. Stretched end to end, the complex dike system would cover 1500 miles, the distance from Boston to Miami—this in a country little larger than Maryland.

But Holland is more than a bulwark against the sea. Just as important, or nearly so, it has produced such men as Erasmus, Hudson, Barents, Tasman, and Leeuwenhoek; and the great painters Bosch, Hals, Rembrandt, Vermeer, Van Gogh, and Mondrian. Further, the Dutch are astonishingly hardworking and thrifty, always making the utmost of their scanty resources.

Despite a high population density (about 900 to the square mile), the 11,000,000 inhabitants of Holland have managed to retain a feeling of space in their lovely farms and villages, and have carefully channeled their love of beauty into the delicate architecture of houses that must, perforce, be crowded into minimum space in their congested cities.

Dutch independence and enterprise, which resulted in the country's eventual freedom from generations of Spanish rule, also led to Holland's development as one of the great maritime powers of the world. Its Eastern empire spread some two thousand miles, from the Indian Ocean to the China Sea, and included Indonesia, Burma, Java, Sumatra and the Celebes. World War II virtually put an end to this empire; Holland was faced not only with the repair of extensive war damage, but also with the repatriation of more than 150,000 Dutch citizens from the Netherlands East Indies, and with the loss of virtually its entire export market.

Nevertheless Dutch economy has been rebuilt and has attained greater prosperity than ever before. More important, the painless absorption of the Dutch Indonesians has proved that people of all races, creeds and colors can live and work together in relative harmony.

THE CANALS OF HOLLAND

(Left) This canal south of Amsterdam is part of the immense network of inland waterways that reaches into every part of the Netherlands. Because of Holland's strategic geographic position, the canals carry an enormous amount of freight, not only domestic, but also from the Rhineland and France, as well as inbound freight via the great port cities of Amsterdam, Rotterdam and Antwerp.

(Below) The Singel Canal (Singelgracht) and some of the stately old homes reflect Amsterdam's past opulence. New housing construction, however, runs to large blocks of modern flats.

(Right) House boats and parked cars along canal edges are familiar and necessary in an area having over 400 bridges connecting fifty miles of canals, all within Amsterdam's limits. Even today, at least one car a week rolls into a canal; it is useful for Dutch drivers to know how to escape from a car resting on a canal bottom.

AMSTERDAM (Centrum)

(Overleaf) The Amstel River cuts through the heart of the city and forks into three small canals just above the Muntplein (Square) and its Munttoren (Mint Tower). In the right center is the Hotel Europe, and the Dolen Hotel. Upper left, the canal ends at the embarkation point from which glass-roofed excursion boats leave. The wide street to the left of the canal is Rokin, a principal shopping center that ends at the Dam Place.

AMSTERDAM (Muntplein)

(Left) This busy intersection is marked by the gilded tower of the Munttoren or Mint Tower, whose bells have been chiming the hours since 1620. Above it is the Kalverstraat, an important shopping street, with the Vroom and Dreesman Department store at the corner. Opposite, a street leads to the Rembrandtplein.

NIEUWMARKT

(Above) The New Market's name is no longer appropriate, for it was a weighing house as far back as 1617. Once part of Amsterdam's town wall, its five-towered building forming one of the gates, it has now been converted into a museum, part of which has been dedicated to Jews martyred during the Nazi occupation.

59

THE ROYAL MUSEUM (Rijksmuseum)

(Above and top right) The imposing esplanade, leading to the Rijksmuseum on the edge of the Singel Canal, puts into proper perspective the reverence the Dutch have for their master painters. The museum itself was first established in 1808 by Louis Bonaparte, though the present building was opened in 1885 and is typical of the heavy architecture of that period. The collection of over 3000 paintings and other works of art here easily places the Rijksmuseum among the greatest in the world.

Appropriately, the museum's Dutch School is represented with thumping emphasis—not only by 15th-century primitives but also by 16th- and 17th-century masters. Rembrandt's "Night Watch" is the most famous painting on display. Among other Dutch painters represented are Vermeer, Jan Steen, Franz Hals, Rubens, Van Dyck and Van Leyden.

MONUMENT TO THE LIBERATION

In the heart of the Dam Place the stark lines of the Monument to the Liberation rise from the concentric circles of its base. Built as a memorial to those Netherlanders who died in the last war, it holds twelve urns, one from each of the eleven provinces of Holland, and one from Indonesia. Each urn holds earth soaked with the blood of a Dutch soldier who lost his life in the war.

DAM PLACE

The Dam Place at the heart of Amsterdam is dominated by the vast Koninklijk Paleis which stands on some 13,650 wooden pilings driven into marshy ground. The Paleis was originally built as a town hall in 1665 but Louis Bonaparte, about 1810, had it converted into a palace. It is still considered an official residence of Queen Juliana, but is rarely used as such except for ceremonial state visits of foreign royalty.

To the right, the Niewe Kerk (New Church) begun in 1408, is new only by comparison to the Oude Kerk (Old Church) which was established in 1306. At the rear of the Niewe Kerk lies the tomb of Admiral De Ruyter, who terrified London in 1667 by blockading the Thames with a fleet of ships which almost nipped in the bud England's future mastery of the sea.

In the upper left is the Westerkerk and, in the foreground, the Monument to the Liberation.

63

TULIPS AND FLOWERS

(Right) Acres of greenhouses on a bulb and flower farm near Rotterdam. Four centuries ago the first tulip bulb was imported from Turkey. And, during the years 1635 to 1640 the development and sale of feathered and flamed varieties became a national craze, and then a wild speculation. A single bulb of a perfect new pattern sold for 1000 florins. Eventually only stringent governmental prohibitions prevented financial disaster. Since then, this astounding tulipomania has of course subsided, and now Dutch farmers export three million bulbs (at a few cents apiece) and thousands of tons of flowers to all parts of the world.

WEST CHURCH (Westerkerk)

(Left) Westerkerk, with its lovely carillon in a 275-foot tower, stands three canals west of the Dam. In a house across the Prinsen Canal and to the right of the church, Anne Frank wrote of her last days before her deportation and death in a German camp.

ROTTERDAM

In the most senseless and wanton destruction of the last war, the city of Rotterdam was virtually leveled one Tuesday (May 14th, 1940) by a skyful of Nazi bombers, who, doing their job thoroughly, destroyed 30,000 buildings, and killed or maimed thousands of civilians.

The horror of this raid stunned the world, but within four days after the destruction of this old and beautiful city, plans were underway for its rebuilding. Reconstruction had to wait until after the liberation, because a new tragedy struck before the Germans were driven out. Retreating, the Nazis dynamited some five miles of piers and wharves in a last-ditch effort to destroy the great port once and for all.

The Dutch themselves have proudly claimed that they were at work rebuilding the port before the rubble had cooled. So successfully have they handled this problem that Rotterdam is now the greatest port in Europe and second only to New York in tonnage handled.

From these ashes and rubble, a new and thoroughly modern city has risen. A vast integrated plan makes maximum use of the large open spaces which resulted from the bombings. The work is far from finished; there are still many sites yet to be filled with new buildings, parks and homes. In the left background is the new Central Station, and on the left is the main new shopping area with a large mall, along with several blocks of apartments. In the upper right are some of the few old buildings which miraculously survived the bombing, the City Hall and Post Office.

66

HAARLEM

Twelve miles from Amsterdam is Haarlem, the fifth largest city in Holland, with a population of 170,000. Though Haarlem is 900 years old, much of its charm dates from 1593, when Lieven de Key, a Flemish architect, designed the master plan for this delightful town.

Haarlem is the city of Franz Hals, the first great painter of his century and country. His handsome commissions came from local guilds and corporations. On the basis of his magnificent representations of their dinner parties, Hals's fortunes prospered, only to decline again, as a result of a reckless life. None of this, however, prevented him from living to be an old man; when he died in 1666, penniless in an almshouse, he was past eighty. Today, that same almshouse is the Franz Hals Museum.

(Left) The enormous church in the upper right is the 15th-century Old St. Bavo's or Grote Kerk. One of the largest churches in Europe, it faces on the Grote Markt, the ancient town square. Here also stands the Vleeshal (meat market) built in 1602, from a design by de Key. Considered to be his masterpiece, the Vleeshal was ridiculed by critics who considered its profusion of detail excessive.

The canal curving through the city is the Spaarn. A mile to the northwest is a memorial (erected in 1950) to a famous hero who never existed, a monument to Dutch courage (in the literal sense) and to the little boy Pieter who stopped the hole in the dike with his finger, and so saved Haarlem from destruction, though he himself died before help came. *(Above)* The new St. Bavo's Church on the city's edge.

GOUDA

(Overleaf) Twelve miles northeast of Rotterdam, Gouda's cheese market is set in a triangular plaza. Through this market pass the wonderful round red-covered cheeses that have made this little town famous. On the lower right is the St. Janskerk, whose sixty-four stained-glass windows are among the finest in the world.

BRUSSELS

(Left) The Church of Laken, close to the Royal Park of Laken and bordering the edge of the city, stands before the Atomium, a permanent symbol of the Brussels Fair of 1958.

BELGIUM

BELGIUM, even smaller than Holland, has a population density almost as great, though it has 2,000,000 fewer inhabitants. Lying as it does between Holland and France, and edged by Germany on the east, Belgium is heavily influenced by its neighbors.

A Belgian citizen regards himself as being either a Fleming or a Walloon. An imaginary line runs from Tournai near the French border almost due east to Aachen in Germany, and this determines the classification: born south of the line and you're a French-speaking Walloon; north and you're Fleming and speak Flemish, a Low German dialect (except for those in the east, who are German-speaking).

Both French and Flemish are official languages; thus many Belgians are bilingual, particularly those from the heavily populated cities of Brussels, Antwerp and Liége. The two languages are used interchangeably in Brussels, the capital, which, architecturally and culturally if not in spirit, seems as Gallic as any city in France.

(Below) On the Plain of Koekelberg overlooking Brussels, and at the end of the tree-lined Boulevard Leopold II, stands the Sacré-Coeur Basilica, better known as the Koekelberg Cathedral. The building is still under construction.

PLACE ROGIER

(*Above*) The Place Rogier in the heart of the city is dominated by a new multi-story office building, one of the highest on the continent, which contrasts sharply with the older more sedate hotels lining the square. To the right of the sky-scraper stands the Palace Hotel, and the Boulevard d'Anvers, leading to the Botanical Gardens and to additional new office buildings in the background.

(*Left*) A small village church near the International Airport at Zavetem.

BRUSSELS

(Above) A hillside residential area just north of the city, and *(below)* the city's center. At the upper left is the 320-foot spire of the 15th-century Town Hall which faces on the Grand Place, whose sides are lined with ancient Guild Houses still occupied by many of the merchant and craft guilds. The Grand Place has many functions. At dawn it serves as wholesale produce market, and then becomes a flower market. By noon the square is usually cleared for normal traffic.

A few streets to the right is the Rue de l'Etuve, on which stands the famous statue of the little boy (Mannekin).

The large building *(left center)* with part of a colonnade showing, is the Bourse (Stock Exchange), and in the foreground is the Church of St. Catherine, built in 1854. The long open area in the foreground is the fish market.

DENMARK

TINY, well-tended Denmark has often been called a fairyland country, and seen from the air, does indeed have a toy-like quality. None of this, however, prevents its people from being thoroughly down to earth: hard-working farmers, sturdy fishermen and sailors, skilled artisans in their tidy cities and towns.

Denmark's maritime tradition is a natural result of its rugged North Sea coastline and its two passages to the Baltic, the Skagerrak and the Kattegat. Most of its land consists of the Jutland Peninsula and almost 500 islands, plus the North Sea Faroe Islands and Greenland.

Denmark's area totals about 17,000 square miles. Some four and a half million people live there, about a fourth of them in the Copenhagen area alone. Köbenhaven (which in Danish means merchant's port) is the country's capital and commercial heart. It is famous for its charm, fine restaurants, hotels, and the delights of its Tivoli Gardens. The food, traditionally Scandinavian, is plentiful and excellent.

Like most north-European cities, Copenhagen originated as a fishing and trading village. In 1167 it was officially established as a city by Bishop Absalon, a national hero who was as good a soldier as he was an ecclesiastic.

Although Denmark has a constitutional government headed by a Prime Minister, the Danes are proud that their monarchy is the oldest in the world today.

THE CITY HALL (Raadhus)

(Right) This graceful building was completed in 1905. The large plaza in front of the Hall is the Raadhusplads; the main street on the left is Hans Christian Andersen's Boulevard, and the intersecting street is the Vesterbrogade. The Tivoli is on the extreme left.

TIVOLI GARDENS

(Above) The Tivoli, across from the Raadhus, is the world-famous amusement park which first opened its gates in 1843. It is estimated that some 200 million people have visited the Tivoli since then. There is something for everyone here: restaurants, a lake, concert halls, open-air theaters, pantomime stages, acrobats, a scenic railway. It even has its own guards, young boys in scarlet uniforms; and summer evenings are made enchanting by the high-tossed bouquets of elaborate fireworks.

COPENHAGEN (Center)

(Left) The large curved street in the foreground is the Köbmagergade, a principal shopping center which ends at Höjbro Plads with its statue of Bishop Absalon. On the left is the Nicholas Church. Across the canal, the spired many-gabled building is the Bourse.

CHRISTIANSBORG PALACE (Royal Castle)

This enormous palace with its 270-foot spire is actually the third to be built on the site. The first Christiansborg Palace was constructed in the reign of Christian IV after a fire had destroyed a large part of the city in 1728. Impressed by the stately Renaissance structures of France and Italy, Christian IV emulated the grand style. His building was destroyed by fire in 1798 and replaced by another, and it too burned, in 1884. However, parts of the building were salvaged and incorporated into this, the third and last Royal Castle of Christiansborg. Not only were many stones from the first two buildings used in the new construction but also rock from 270 Danish villages.

A statue of Frederik VII, in whose reign the Danish Constitution was enacted in 1849, stands directly before the Palace. The building now houses the Danish Parliament, the Foreign Office

and the Supreme Court of Justice. In the large curved section on the left are the Royal Arsenal Museum and the Royal Danish Theater Museum. The enclosed area is the Castle Square with the Royal Gate immediately behind it.

The National Museum is across the Frederiksholmns Canal, behind the Royal Gate, and in the right foreground is the tower of the Nicholas Church. The canal in the foreground constitutes part of the Gammel Strand, the city's fish market.

KRONBORG CASTLE

At Elsinore (Helsingör), a seaport on the east coast of Zeeland about twenty-four miles from Copenhagen stands Kronborg Castle, completed in 1577 by Frederik II, from Dutch designs. It was a royal residence, also a marine and customs collecting station, and was used by Shakespeare as the setting for *Hamlet*. It is now an international tourist attraction; every summer actors from all over the world take part in productions in the castle courtyard.

Recently Elsinore has provided the décor for other tragic, heroic events. During the Nazi occupation, Danish Jews were hidden in Elsinore homes until they could be escorted across the frozen Oresund to safety, at Halsingborg in Sweden. After the war, the people of Elsinore erected a monument (Svea Column) in memory and appreciation of Swedish help given to the Danish people during the Occupation. The Danes are proud, and well they might be, that they were able to smuggle out their entire Jewish population.

Other than the rescue of Jewish citizens, many other stories of Danish resistance are well remembered. Though Denmark was occupied early in the war, and subjected to terrible brutality, the Germans never quite managed to subdue the Danes. Many Nazi soldiers mysteriously vanished in that tiny and peaceful country.

THE FARMS OF DENMARK

Zeeland, the island on which Copenhagen and Elsinore are located, is flat and has rich fertile soil. From this lush earth come Denmark's great food products: fine cheeses, milk and butter, the grains for Danish beer (exported in vast quantities), and the fat cattle and swine which contribute beef and delicious hams to an already excellent Danish cuisine.

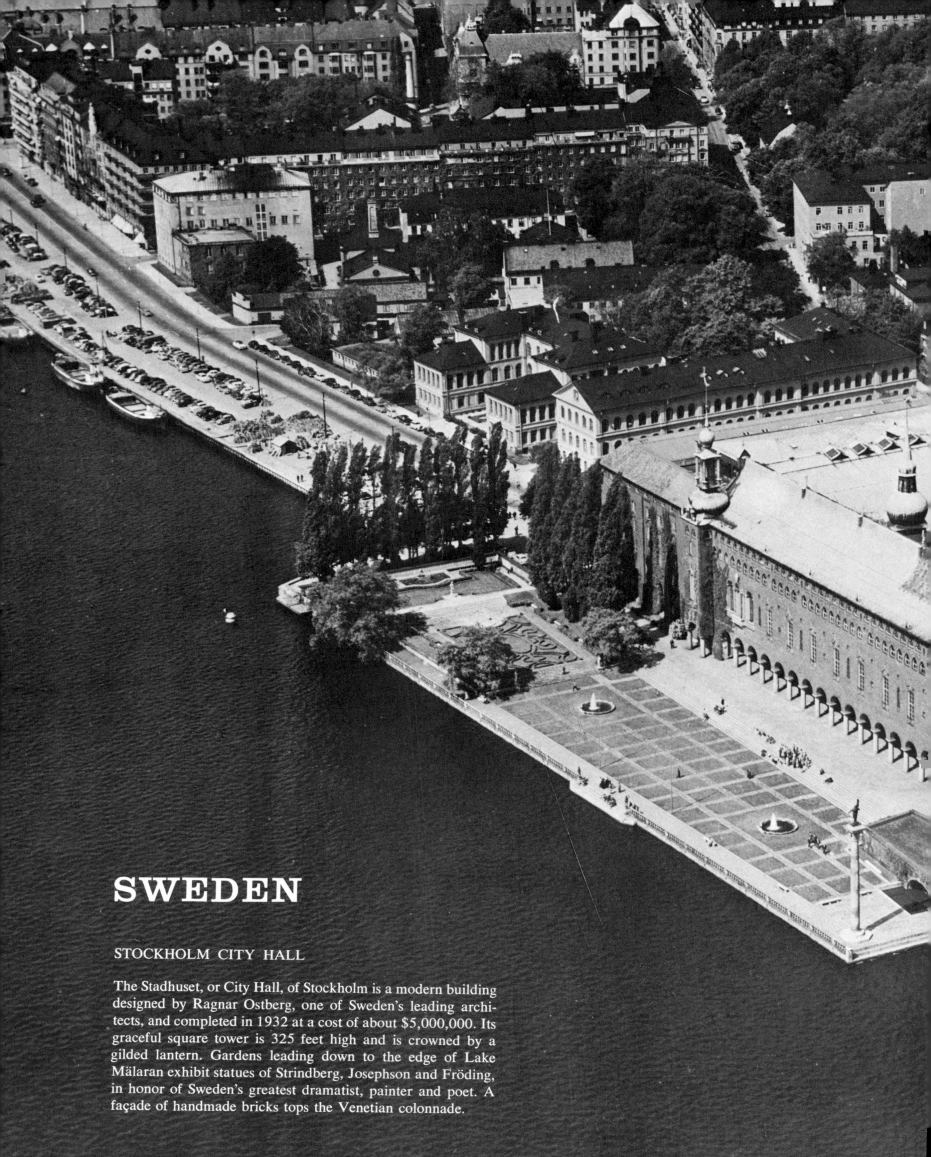

SWEDEN

STOCKHOLM CITY HALL

The Stadhuset, or City Hall, of Stockholm is a modern building designed by Ragnar Ostberg, one of Sweden's leading architects, and completed in 1932 at a cost of about $5,000,000. Its graceful square tower is 325 feet high and is crowned by a gilded lantern. Gardens leading down to the edge of Lake Mälaran exhibit statues of Strindberg, Josephson and Fröding, in honor of Sweden's greatest dramatist, painter and poet. A façade of handmade bricks tops the Venetian colonnade.

SWEDEN

ONE of the largest countries in Europe, Sweden is also one of the oldest. Its lands stretch a thousand miles, from the Baltic Sea to the wastes within the Arctic Circle. Its earliest settlements date as far back as 3000 B.C., and its Viking exploits were already legendary by the 8th century. By the 14th century, Sweden had begun to take cohesive shape, and its first constitution was adopted. During this period, however, Sweden fell under Danish rule: in 1520 the Massacre of Stockholm took place, and the leaders of a Swedish independence movement were executed by Denmark's king. Nevertheless, later that winter a successful revolt, led by Gustav Eriksson of the Vasa family, established Sweden's national state under the powerful reign of the Vasa Dynasty.

The Reform came in 1527 and the Swedish Church separated from Rome, to become Lutheran. This did not bring peace to Sweden, which continued to fight off and on for centuries afterward, until 1812. She has not fought a war since that date.

In our times, a policy of neutrality backed by a highly modernized military machine has assured Sweden of independence. Sweden today is a constitutional monarchy and a world leader in social reforms.

ENGELBREKT CHURCH

This church stands on the Karlavagen in the northern part of the city. Behind it is the Birjer Jarlsgaten, named after the founder of Stockholm.

86

STOCKHOLM

Stockholm, was already known as a trading town about 1250. One of its earliest military chiefs, the legendary Count Birger, later fortified the neighboring islands of Staden, Helgeandsholmen and Riddarholmen. Eventually the city grew to include the thirteen islands from Lake Mälaren to the entrance of the Baltic Sea. Its population has grown to almost a million now. Stockholm suffered a series of great fires; the last in 1857, cleared the city of its wooden houses. Most of the replacements were made of stone.

VASA CHURCH

(Above) The Vasa Church, in the northwest part of the city, contains the beautiful 18th-century altar which formerly was in Upsala Cathedral.

GRAND HOTEL

(Below) On the waterfront and in the city's heart, the Grand Hotel, one of the finest in Europe, overlooks a Strömmen quay across from the Royal Palace.

NYBROPLAN

(*Above*) Facing the Berzelii Park on the quay of the Nybroviken inlet, the Royal Dramatic Theater commands that intersection of Birjer Jarssgaten and the Strandvägen where the excursion boats are moored.

NORDIC MUSEUM

(*Right*) The Nordiska Museet, at the east end of the Strandvägen, contains a large collection of Nordic artifacts.

KARLA PLAN

The long winters of Sweden and the high density of Stockholm's population make apartment living a requirement for most of the city's inhabitants. Central heating, elevators and all other necessities of modern urban living have long been in operation in Stockholm, and the city planners and architects have not forgotten the spiritual necessities of a big city: wide boulevards, parks, trees and shrubs.

Apartments on the Karla Plan, on the city's northern edge, make the most of their available space. The older buildings are covered with ivy and, wherever possible, trees have been planted.

Facing the circle, on the edge of the second street from the left, is the building where Sweden's most famous dramatist, August Strindberg, lived.

91

DROTTNINGHOLM PALACE

The summer residence of the Royal family, Drottningholm Palace stands on Lake Mälaren, only a short drive from the heart of Stockholm. It was built from 1662 to 1681 in the style of the French Renaissance. Other than the royal apartments and historical mementoes, it houses a splendid theater built by Gustav III and a theater museum. Surrounding the palace on three sides lies a carefully patterned park. In it, you'll find a tiny Chinese pagoda, built as a summer house by King Adolf Frederick in the 18th century for his Queen.

The palace can be reached by steamer, in less than an hour, from a quay near the City Hall, and it is open to the public whenever the Royal Family is not in residence.

93

FRANCE

AS SURELY as Paris is the heart of France, so surely is it the heart of the Western World. First of all, and last, Paris is a living myth, and like all myths, easily absorbs all those who come under its influence, no matter what their nationality. Paris is unique in this: unlike other cities one may love, Paris does not leave your love unrequited, or so at least you feel convinced. Paris in all its beauty, in its magnificence and in its neighborly intimacy, is made for human beings as it is made by them. The personal relationship that exists between Paris and

the Parisian extends to the visitor. The true Parisian outside of Paris is easy enough to spot: he is at best restless, at worst wretchedly unhappy.

Too, where is the love for Paris and all it stands for—grace, elegance, culture, ambience—expressed so passionately as in the French towns and villages far from the loveliest of cities? It was Montaigne who said: *"Paris a mon coeur dès mon enfance. Je ne suis français que par cette grande cité, grande surtout et incomparable, la gloire de la France, et l'un des* *plux beaux ornements du monde."* There is in truth no country like France, no city comparable to Paris.

(Above) The River Seine, approaching Paris from the west, cuts through the heart of the city, past the Eiffel Tower. In the center foreground is the fashionable Sixteenth Arrondissement. Lower left, the Avenue Paul Doumer leads to the Place du Trocadéro and the Palais de Chaillot. *Upper left,* the Basilica of the Sacred Heart dominates the city from Montmartre.

THE ETOILE

To fly over the Etoile is immediately to understand the reason for its name: a huge twenty-four-point star is clearly defined by inlaid paving blocks. Twelve of these points lead to the twelve avenues radiating from the great hub of the Arc de Triomphe. Starting with the Champs Elysées (the large Avenue directly behind the Arc's main archway) and rotating clockwise, we have Marceau, Iena, Kléber, Victor Hugo, Foch, Grand Armée, Carnot, Mac-Mahon, Wagram, Hoche and Friedland.

But the days of Napoleon's glory are long since past and, aside from its splendid perspectives, the Etoile usually means only one thing to pedestrian and motorist alike: the apparition of sudden death. Anyone, whether on foot or in a car, attempting to negotiate the Etoile during rush hour is as brave as those hardened traffic champions, the Parisian taxi drivers—or braver, for the *chauffeur*s often tend to take the Etoile's two small encircling streets (Rue de Presbourg or Rue de Tilsit) to avoid the roaring maelstrom.

Napoleon ordered the Etoile built to commemorate his victories. On the design of Jean François Chalgrin, its construction began in 1806 and was completed thirty years later. On the walls of the Arch are carved the names of the 384 generals under Napoleon's command, with the list of their 96 victories. In 1920 an eternal flame was lighted under the arch in memory of France's unknown soldier in World War I. On national holidays a huge tricolor hangs there, illuminated at night by red, white and blue spotlights.

Standing on a little rise of ground, the 160-foot-high arch dominates the western end of the city. An inside stairway and elevator rise to the roof of the arch, where you will be rewarded by a spectacular, if splendidly confusing, view of Paris's miles of roof-tops.

AVENUE DES CHAMPS ELYSEES

Few choose to dispute the French claim that the Champs Elysées is the world's most beautiful avenue. For a mile and a quarter, from the Place de la Concorde *(upper right)* to the Etoile, this graceful street, with its border of chestnut trees, provides an enchanting, if somewhat crowded, promenade for millions of French-men and visitors alike. The Champs Elysées, actually beginning at the Concorde, runs west through a gracious park with flower beds, fountains, coffee houses and restaurants, goes past the Rond-Point, where the Avenues Montaigne and Franklin Roosevelt intersect, and from there its run is clear to the Etoile, past stylish shops, hotels, restaurants and sidewalk cafés which have made the Champs Elysées renowned in every country in the world.

PLACE DE LA CONCORDE AND CHURCH OF THE MADELEINE

(Left) Between the Tuileries Gardens and the Champs Elysées, the Place de la Concorde has had a checkered history. During the Revolution, the guillotines there beheaded Louis XVI, Marie Antoinette, Robespierre, Danton, and many others. Looking forward to a roseate future, the name Concorde was given to the Place immediately after the Reign of Terror.

At each of the four corners are paired statues symbolizing France's eight principal cities. They represent *(starting upper left, clockwise),* Marseilles, Bordeaux, Nantes, Brest, Rouen, Lille, Strasbourg, Lyons. Dead center stands the Obelisk, a 75-foot shaft brought from Thebes in 1831 as a gift to Louis Philippe from the Viceroy of Egypt. As well, there are two Roman fountains in the center of the Place, the Font des Fleuves *(foreground)* and the Font des Mers. The entrance to the Champs Elysées is far right.

(Above) These two colonnaded structures *(foreground)* were constructed in 1732 as reception buildings for distinguished visitors and have been Parisian landmarks ever since. With some qualifica-

tion, this original purpose remains fulfilled: the building on the left houses the Hotel Crillon, one of the most venerable and elegant hotels in Paris; the building on the right is the Ministry of the Marine. As a small part of the clean-up program now being carried out in Paris, both have just been scrubbed clean of two hundred years' accumulation of grime, and the soft yellow-pink color of the old stonework is clearly visible.

Intersecting these two buildings, Rue Royale leads directly to the handsome Church of the Madeleine. In classic Roman style, with its eight frontal Corinthian columns, the Madeleine is one of the most fashionable churches in Paris. Construction was begun in 1764, but Napoleon altered the building to make it a monument to his army. It was restored as a church and completed in 1842. Just as fashionable but, alas, astronomically expensive, the west side of Rue Royale houses "Chez Maxim" where, almost any night of the week, you can watch the most elegant Parisians dispatch exquisite dinners produced by some of France's greatest chefs.

101

Like a great ship, the Île de la Cité rides the Seine with the Île St. Louis towed from its stern. Bridges appear as gangways, leading to shops and offices of

Forbidding fortress, the Conciergerie through the centuries imprisoned the accused in its towers and dungeons. The medieval building takes its name from its first housekeeper, the concierge of the royal household, who acted as jailer.

Waiting room for the guillotine: During the French Revolution, guards herded prisoners into a barred section of this medieval gallery in the Conciergerie. There and in fetid cells, they listened for the dread call to execution on the Right Bank.

Condemned queen, Marie Antoinette spent 11 weeks in the Conciergerie before her execution on October 16, 1793. Forgiving her foes, the 37-year-old aristocrat met her fate with dignity.

COURTESY MUSÉE CARNAVALET, PARIS

window, newspaper stretched wide, cigar gled alertly upward, long jaw jutting.

"Jim," I hollered. "You available?"

He grinned and beckoned. James Jone 46 one of the most successful of Ameri novelists, has lived on the Paris islands ten years (page 711).

As I moved toward his door he cal "Wait, I'm coming down. I feel like walki We turned into a side street and crossec the north branch of the Seine.

"I love this doggone island," he said words to that effect). "There's nothing lik Quiet. Great people. The shopping stre like a village market. You ought to see fish store after dark. It's like a painting."

On the quay he stopped suddenly pointed. "See that crummy old launch by

the Right Bank (left) and to cafes and colleges on the Left. In this aerial view, the metropolis stretches to the Vincennes forest five miles to the southeast. France measures road distances from a zero-mile marker in the square below Notre Dame's twin towers. In a gaping excavation in the square, archeologists labor to bare Roman ruins, tangible reminders of the capital's ancient past.

The Flower Seed Growers
Gardening's Color

By ROBERT DE ROOS   *Photographs by JACK FIELL*

I N THE COURSE of a 7,500-mile odyssey
through the fields, laboratories, and
greenhouses of the American flower seed
industry, I met most of the small packet of
seedsmen who are responsible for the beauty
and hardiness of today's flowers. They are
a unique band, men in whom patience,
persistence, and pride mingle in roughly
equal proportions.

They are not really Big Business—
the total retail value of their product
is only about $30,000,000 a year.
Nevertheless, it is hard to think of an
industry that yields more beauty per ounce.

Behind the steady improvement of garden
flowers lie thousands of test plantings, years
of careful selection and crossing of varieties,
and a determined search for mutants—
plants with new characteristics. The work
is endless and expensive. Most of it is
done by the major flower companies that

EMBRYO OF BEAUTY, *a geraniu*
seed, enlarged 12 times, will
sprout and bloom in the spring
Before packaging, growers wil
scarify it to hasten germinatior
and remove the wispy tail, a
device of nature for scattering
seeds in the wind. To create a
new variety of petunia, Gloria
Herrera (inset) vacuums
pollen from a parent plant in
a California seedsman's
greenhouse. KODACHROMES © N.G.S.

THE LOUVRE

Formerly one of the greatest of all palaces, now probably the world's most renowned museum, the Louvre is the work of many kings and architects, a mélange of styles and buildings modified and brought into relative harmony over three centuries of time and weather.

Before Nôtre-Dame was erected, there was an old fortress on the site of the present east court of the Louvre. Traces of it are under the pavement. Philippe Auguste, about the year 1200, converted the fortress into a palace, which by the time of Charles V, c.1375, had become a fairy-tale castle of countless turrets and battlements and a grand stairway lined with statues. But during the hardships of the Hundred Years War it was neglected, then deserted, and it nearly fell into ruins. Not until the middle of the 16th century, under Catherine de Médicis and Henry II, was the present construction begun—and then in the richly ordered style of the Italian-French Renaissance. Immense wings and courtyards were added by successive monarchs until the time of Napoleon III, when it reached nearly as far as the Palais de Tuileries and comprised the vastest architectural ensemble in the world.

After Napoleon III was deposed; mobs burned the Tuileries to the ground; and its site was converted, later, into the present always-delightful Jardin des Tuileries, which Parisians and tourists enjoy fully as much as they do the Louvre itself.

Looking eastward over the Tuileries Gardens, the Arch of the Carrousel occupies the center; and the long wings, along the Seine, contain the Grande Galerie. The Cour du Louvre is in the rear and includes the oldest portions.

The street in the lower left is the Rue St. Honoré, one of the richest shopping centers in the world. The cross street is Avenue du Général Lemonier. The arcaded Rue de Rivoli runs parallel to the wing of the Louvre, and to the far left (center) you can make out the southwest corner of the Théâtre Française.

Across the river: the Left Bank and *(top left)* the Ile de la Cité.

Today, the seven museums of the Louvre hold a total of 200,000 works of art, some of the best-known are the Mona Lisa, Manet's "Olympia," Degas' "Absinthe," and Renoir's "The Swing." There are many pictures by Flemish and Italian masters, and a large collection of ancient sculpture, including the "Venus de Milo," and "The Winged Victory of Samothrace." Forty acres of buildings are set down on another fifty acres of gardens, with an unparalleled view of the Tuileries, Place de la Concorde, and the Champs Elysées.

LOUVRE—OPERA—INSTITUT DE FRANCE

(Left) Near the middle of the north wing of the Louvre is the broad Avenue d'l'Opéra. The Paris Opera *(above)* built in 1874, has a tremendous stage, a tremendous stairway and, of course, tremendous prestige—but a seating capacity of only about 2000.

In the Louvre's foreground stands the colonnade, designed by Perrault and built in 1670; and the bridge crossing the Seine is the Pont des Arts. In the left foreground is the Institut de France, which is made up of the five Academies of France. One of these, the Académie Française, created in 1635 by Richelieu to edit the official French dictionary, has a membership limited to forty. The Institut's other academies are the Académie des Beaux Arts, Académie des Inscriptions et Belles Lettres, Académie des Sciences, and the Académie des Sciences Morales et Politiques.

THE EIFFEL TOWER

(Right) In the Champ-de-Mars, directly across the Seine from the Palace of Chaillot, the steel tower rises more than a thousand feet (with the newly installed TV antennae), and is the third tallest building in the world. Designed by Alexandre Eiffel, and built for the Paris exposition of 1889, it provoked cries of outrage from the French press but has since then become *the* worldwide symbol of Paris herself. Elevators take visitors to an observation deck 902 feet above ground. There are restaurants on the lower level and a bar at the top. The view from up there is overwhelming, unforgettable, enough to make a prospective suicide change his mind.

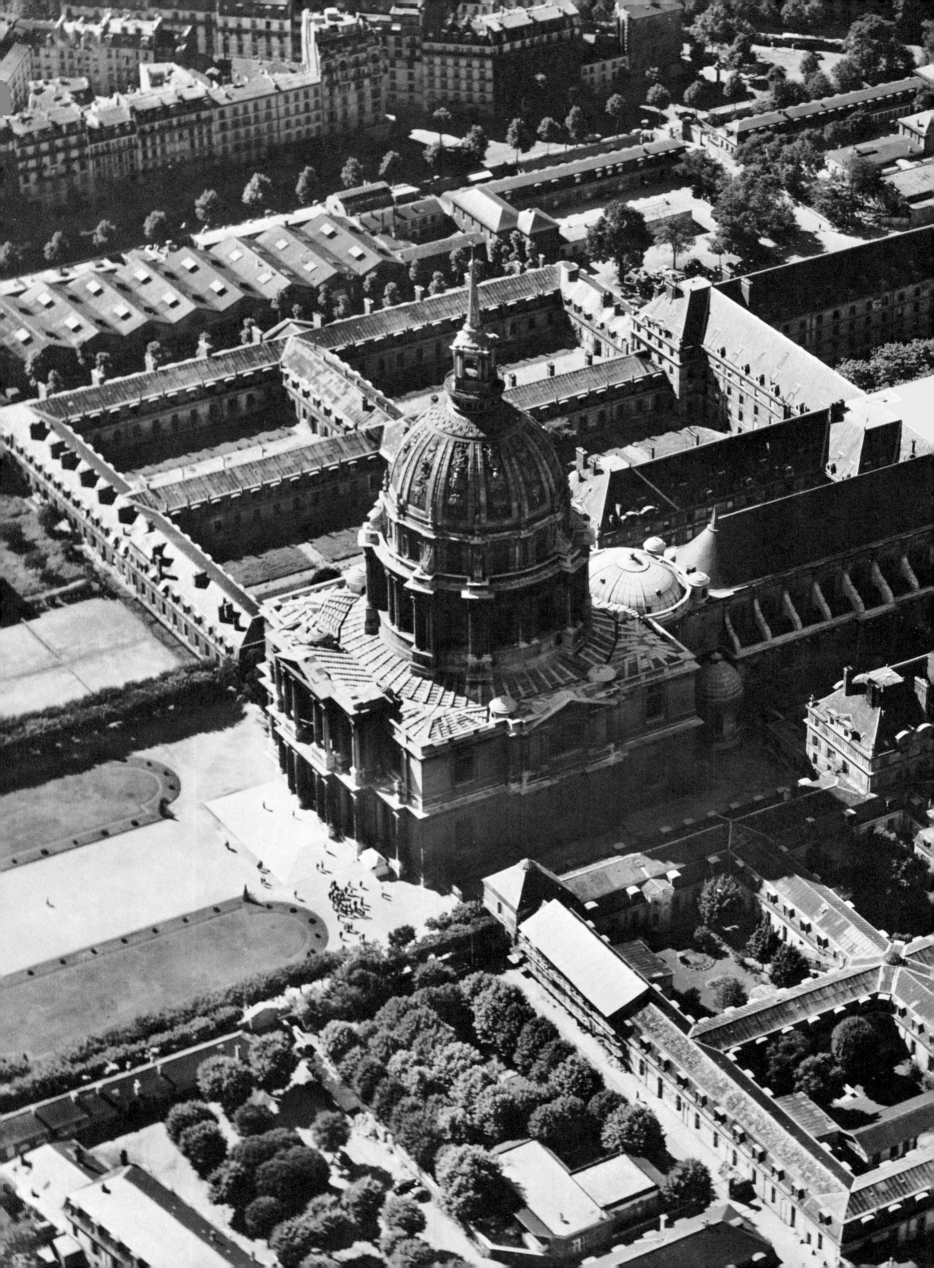

HOTEL DES INVALIDES

At the south end of the Esplanade des Invalides (south side of the Pont Alexandre III), the Hôtel des Invalides dominates the wide square. This enormous building was begun in 1671 by Louis XIV as a home for disabled soldiers. It once housed almost 7000 pensioners, but there are now only some 100 veterans of World War I there. The building has always been used by the Army and is the headquarters of Paris's Military Governor.

It is Napoleon's tomb under the vast gilt-covered lead dome that constitutes the principal attraction and the focus. The dome, the highest in Paris, was designed by J. Hardouin-Mansart and was constructed in 1706 as an addition to the Royal Chapel of St. Louis (behind the dome). The inner crypt is shaped like a Greek cross, and Napoleon's remains are protected by six coffins, each within another, in a massive sarcophagus of polished red marble. At the tomb's entry a heavy door protects the crypt, and two large statues, Military and Civil Power, stand guard.

Behind the Chapel the main sections of the building form a series of courts which cluster around the Cour d'Honneur, onto which the fine Musée de L'Armée faces.

In the upper right, the north façade of the Invalides stretches for 700 feet across the Esplanade.

107

LEFT BANK—ALEXANDER III BRIDGE

(Above) To the right of the Pont Alexandre III with its rococo gilt statues, lies the Quai d'Orsay, home of the French Foreign Office, and the Bourbon Palace, in which the National Assembly meets. In the right foreground is the Church of Ste. Clotilde, where César Franck was organist for thirty years.

GRAND PALAIS AND PETIT PALAIS

(Right) These two exhibition halls, overlooking the Seine and west of the Place de la Concorde, are modern, though classic in design. The Grand Palais is used for large expositions, such as the International Auto Show each fall, and the Petit Palais for special art shows as well as for its permanent collection. The bridges seen here are: Pont Alexandre III, right, then Pont de la Concorde, Pont de Solférino, Pont Royal, and Pont du Carrousel.

HOTEL DE VILLE

(Upper right) The City Hall of Paris is a replica of the original, built in 1532, which was destroyed by rioting mobs during the Commune of 1871. The square in front of the Hall was until 1830 called the Place de Grève, and has a gruesome history as a place of public execution. Behind the Hôtel de Ville is the Church of St. Gervais, which has still some elements of the purest flamboyant Gothic in France.

In the foreground is the Tour St. Jacques, all that remains of the Church of St. Jacques-la-Boucherie. At the right is the Place du Châlet and the Théâtre Sarah Bernhardt. The Seine's two islands, Ile de la Cité and Ile Saint Louis, are in the upper right. The bridges, starting on the right are Pont Nôtre-Dame, Pont d'Arcole, Pont Louis Philippe and Pont Marie. Connecting the two islands is the Pont St. Louis.

PALACE OF JUSTICE

(*Above*) On the west end of the Ile de la Cité, the Palace of Justice straddles the width of the island. In its center is one of Paris's loveliest gothic structures, the Sainte Chapelle, which was finished in 1284 by Louis IX. Its stained glass ranks with that of Chartres as the best in the world.

The Palace dates from the 10th century; and every king subsequently extended it, until it reached its present size around 1814. The Courts of Justice sat here during the Reign of Terror and filled the Conciergerie with thousands of victims. Among its occupants were Marie-Antoinette, Mme. du Barry, and the leaders of the Revolution, Danton and Robespierre. Now a museum, the Conciergerie's present entrance is between the second and third tower on the north side.

In the foreground is the Pont Neuf, the oldest bridge in Paris. It was built between 1578 and 1604, during which time it was lined with shops and houses. Where the bridge crosses the western tip of the Ile, the statue of Henry IV faces heroically toward the Place Dauphine. Behind the Palace of Justice, is the Prefecture of Police and the domed Tribunal of Commerce. The Marché aux Fleurs, the Hotel Dieu, and Nôtre-Dame are directly behind the Tribunal.

In the upper right the Panthéon rises on the Mont de Paris, highest part of the Left Bank. Like the Tomb of Napoleon, the Panthéon is designed in the form of a Greek Cross, and the massive dome is 270 feet high. It was originally erected to commemorate a supposed 5th-century church of Ste. Geneviève, the special saint of Paris. In 1791 the Assembly directed that it be used as the burial place for France's distinguished citizens. Entombed there are Rousseau, Voltaire, Victor Hugo, Emile Zola and Louis Braille.

Surrounding the Panthéon on every side, Paris's old Latin Quarter, whose center is the Sorbonne on the long axis of the Boulevard St. Michel, has provided a way of life, as well as backdrop, for generations of students from all over the world, students who can trace their vocational lineage back to Aquinas, Abélard, Villon, and Montaigne. The Latin Quarter, along with its inhabitants, has all the intoxicating atmosphere of eternal youth, all the familiarity of a well-thumbed book.

CATHEDRAL OF NÔTRE-DAME

Nôtre-Dame de Paris, if not the most beautiful French cathedral, is certainly the most famous. Napoleon was crowned there. Victor Hugo used it as setting for his *Hunchback of Nôtre-Dame.* The south tower houses a 13-ton bell cast in 1686. The panoramic views of Paris from platforms 220 feet above the Parvis (the square in front of the Cathedral) are superb. Millions of tourists and Parisians have trudged up those 387 steps to enjoy these classic vistas.

This site on the Ile de la Cité, which divides the Seine, has been occupied by churches since the 6th century when the Cathedral of St. Etienne stood here. A Cathedral of Nôtre-Dame was subsequently built farther east in Paris about the 9th century, but eventually both churches were consolidated into the present structure. Pope Alexander III laid the cornerstone in 1163 and it was, for the most part, finished before 1300. Architecturally the cathedral is important too because it was the first cathedral to make use of flying buttresses to support the massive roof. The earlier Church of St. Germain-des-Prés had employed *"arcs-boutants"* on a smaller scale. The famous gargoyles, half man, half beast, by Viollet-le-Duc, adorn the towers and rims of the building, and the base of the 312-foot central spire, the *flèche,* is adorned with statues of saints, prophets and chimeras.

The south porch *(above)* contains the Portal of St. Etienne and a magnificent rose window.

Despite its ornate Gothic exterior, the interior is surprisingly simple, beautifully proportioned and spacious. The massive nave can hold 9000 people, and on such special occasions as the Liberation of Paris, 13,000 have crowded in for Mass.

The curved street behind the cathedral is the Rue Chanoinesse, one of the oldest in Paris. In the foreground is the Pont au Double, crossing the south branch of the Seine as it swirls around the Ile and along the Left Bank's Quai de Montebello.

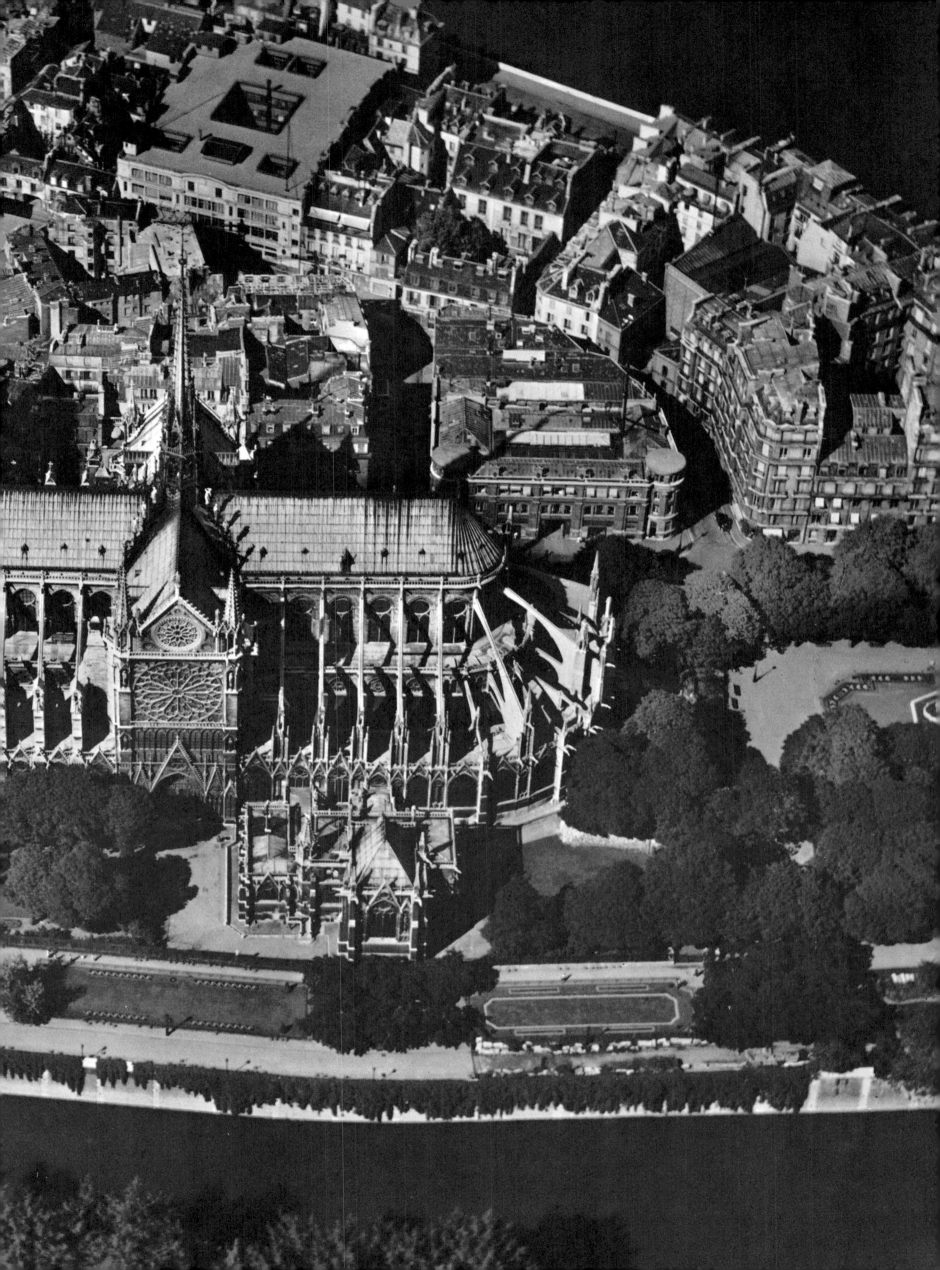

Artists Love to Sketch Street Scenes in Montmartre, a Paris Hilltop, Where Visitors Dine at Sidewalk Cafes

Traffic-dodging waiters, crossing the street, carry tasty dishes from three restaurants to tree- and umbrella-shaded tables in the Place du Tertre. The basilica of Sacré Cœur, with its gleaming domes, overlooks Paris from a height of 335 feet above the Seine.

49

Kodachrome by Willard R. Culver

A Poem in Structural Steel, the Eiffel Tower Arches Skyward over Paris

Only New York's Empire State and Chrysler Buildings top Gustave Eiffel's 984-foot wonder of the 1889 Paris Exhibition. These visitors tread the esplanade of the Palace of Chaillot, where Trocadéro Palace once stood.

SACRÉ-COEUR AND MONTMARTRE

(Left) The Basilica of the Sacred Heart is, after the Eiffel Tower, Paris's most visible landmark, and many contend its ugliest. Sacré-Coeur's modern Romanesque-Byzantine architecture is, indeed, out of place, almost bizarre, high on its hill in Montmartre. The hill itself has always been one of the military keys to the city: take Montmartre and Paris is yours. During the Revolution of 1871 the Communards held it for almost two months, but in those days there was no Basilica to win or defend, because construction of the building did not begin until 1875. It has served as a church since 1891, though it was not consecrated until 1919.

However, it is the area around Sacré-Coeur, Montmartre itself, that draws those armies of tourists every year. Before 1900, many poorer artists and writers, attracted by cheap lodgings, cafés, and restaurants, made Montmartre the creative center of Paris for some thirty years; then, for inscrutable reasons, they moved to Montparnasse and stayed there until 1939, to move again, after the War, to Saint Germain-des-Prés.

Later, the area below the Butte began to develop as the amusement center of the city, and as night-clubs and dives spread along the Boulevard Rochechouart (the large boulevard below the church) and into Pigalle *(left),* hordes of tourists invaded the hilltop seeking what their very presence in such numbers prevented them from finding: the atmosphere that Toulouse-Lautrec and Utrillo had depicted.

Some of the old flavor still exists. The Place du Tertre, except on weekends, is still what it was 70 years ago; and the art galleries, curio shops, bars and cafés afford relative pleasures to those who come to savor the romance of a Montmartre—enforced poverty is *never* amusing—no longer extant.

(Above) To the left of the Basilica is the tiny church of St. Pierre-de-Montmartre, built in 1747 to honor St. Denis. To the left of the church, and slightly below, is the Place du Tertre, just above the street which winds up from Pigalle past the famous "Lapin Agile" café. There, the crowds still jam in, to sip cognac, hear poets and singers, and perhaps sadly to remember that Picasso, Apollinaire, Breton, and le Douanier Rousseau sat together on these same benches not many years ago.

115

VERSAILLES

Louis XIV, always suspicious of Paris and apprehensive of working class mobs, felt that the ten miles separating Versailles and the Palais Royale represented a reasonable safety zone, and therefore decided to build this enormous palace as a lasting monument to his reign. Construction began in 1661 and was completed in 1682. The parks and gardens, which took some fifty years to complete, were laid out by Le Nôtre, and 30,000 workmen were employed on the project; a court entourage of almost 20,000 people came to live there.

The dimensions are literally king-sized. The main façade is over a third of a mile in length and has 375 windows. The parks contain lakes, canals, and 140 fountains. Whole forests, shaped and pruned, spread over 250 acres. The Orangerie contained 3000 exotic shrubs.

But over a century later the distance from Paris hardly deterred the women of Les Halles who led the march to the palace on October 6th, 1789. They massacred the bodyguard and captured Louis XVI and Marie Antoinette, bringing them back to Paris.

Through all of France's subsequent history, Versailles has been important. Napoleon lived there, as did (briefly) most of France's few remaining kings. It was occupied by a Russian Czar (Alexander) and was the scene of the coronation of William I of Prussia as Emperor of Germany. The Republic was proclaimed by the Assembly in Versailles' Opera House in 1875. The Treaty of Versailles, ending the First World War (and, many hold, beginning the Second), was signed in the Galerie des Glaces; and the Allies used the building as their headquarters in 1944 and 1945 after the liberation of Paris.

To the right, the Cour Royale contained the royal apartments and the connecting Galerie de Glaces (Hall of Mirrors). The queen's apartment was on the near side. The royal ministers were housed on both sides of the large court behind. Beyond the gate the vast Place d'Armes is now used for parking.

117

FONTAINEBLEAU

As Versailles is symbolic of Louis XIV so Fontainebleau bears Napoleon's lasting stamp. Because of his outright distaste for the aura that surrounded Versailles, Bonaparte preferred Fontainebleau even though it was built centuries before his time.

Set in a 40,000-acre forest preserve, the Château is an excellent example of the Italian-Renaissance grand style. François I, who was responsible for its initial design, imported many Italian artists and craftsmen, including Cellini, Primaticcio and Rosso, to convert the old fortress built by Louis VII on the site of a 12th-century hunting lodge.

Yet with the passage of time, the great palace has retained a distinct feeling of intimacy, perhaps because each succeeding king added to it, not a wing or gallery, but a complete royal unit with the sharp imprint of its particular creator—this in contrast to the vast single complex that comprises Versailles and renders it impersonal.

Napoleon's association with Fontainebleau reached its climax when Pope Pius VII arrived there in 1804 to crown him Emperor. The Pope's own association with Fontainebleau was later to be involuntary, for he was brought there after his abduction from Rome in 1812. Kept a prisoner for a year and a half he finally consented to the annulment of Napoleon's marriage to Josephine and to the renunciation of his own temporal power. (The latter decision he later repudiated.)

During World War II Fontainebleau served as headquarters for the German forces of occupation until its liberation by General Patton in August 1944.

The large courtyard on the left is the Cour du Cheval Blanc (Court of the White Horse) which later became known as the Cour des Adieux: Napoleon stood on the horse-shoe staircase when he reviewed his Imperial Guard before his exile to Elba and on his return.

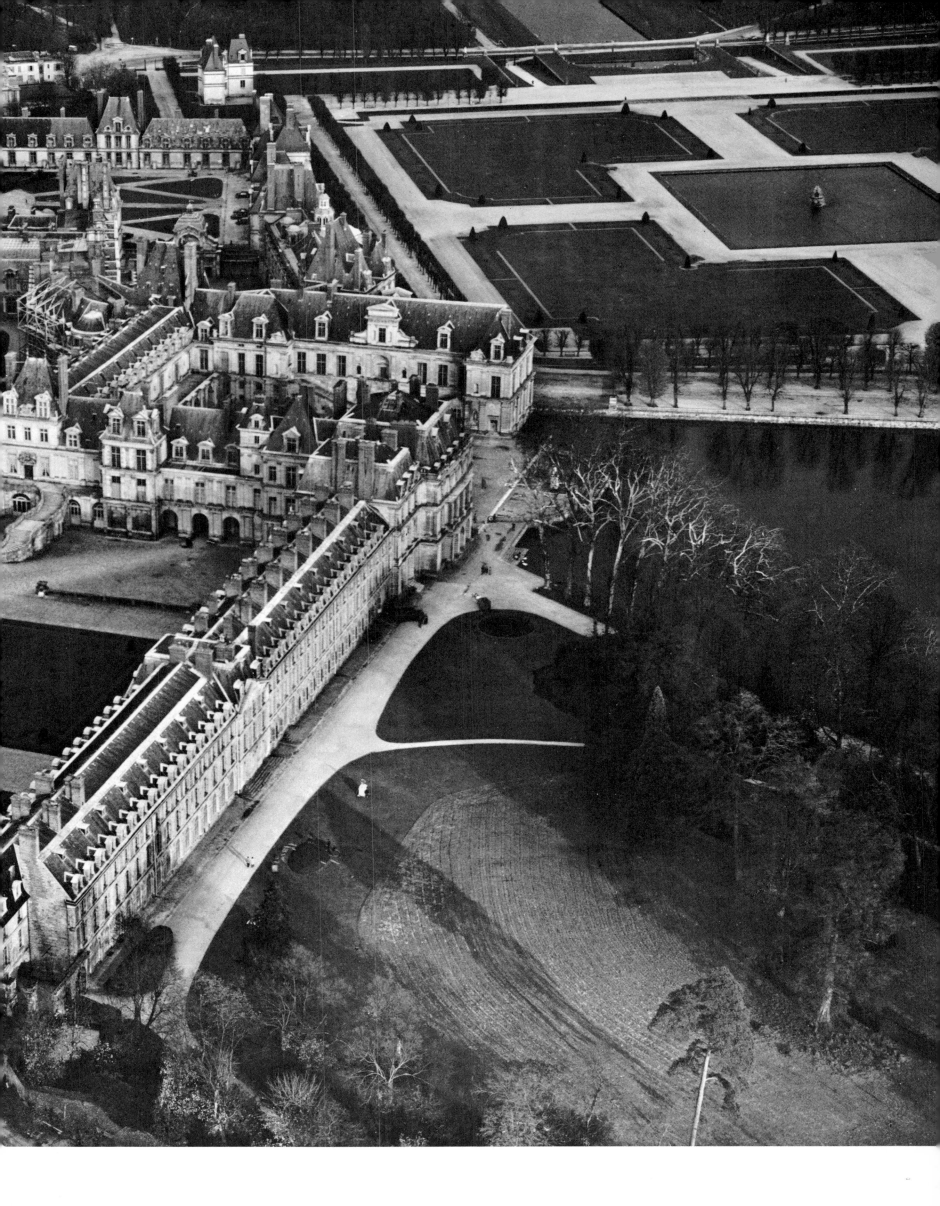

CHANTILLY

(Left) Twenty-five miles north of Paris, near the town renowned for its lacework and horseracing, and one excellent dessert, the Château of Chantilly sparkles in its setting of formal ponds and gardens. The happy union of 16th-century Petit Château and 19th-century Grand Château has produced one of France's finest castles.

Now a museum, it first belonged to Henry II of Montmorency, who was executed 1632, and at that time the title passed to the Grand Condé, whose mother was a Montmorency. The family's last descendant, the Duc d'Aumale, bequeathed the Château and its art treasures to the French Academy on the condition that the collection should never leave the Château.

Here are paintings by Giotto, Botticelli, and Raphael; Memling and Van Dyck; Clouet and Fouquet; as well as the enchanting illuminated manuscript, *Les Très Riches Heures du Duc de Berri.*

COMPIEGNE

(Above) Ranking only after Versailles and Fontainebleau, Compiègne, though built by Louis XV, is actually most noted for its collection of Empire furniture.

Here, Napoleon married his second wife, Marie-Louise of Austria. Later the Château served as setting for the lavish entertainments of Empress Eugénie, wife of Napoleon III.

The town, which is forty-six miles northeast of Paris, dates back to Charlemagne. Joan of Arc was imprisoned here. Nearby on a special spur built for the occasion stands the railway car in which the World War I Armistice was signed. It was also in this car, in 1940, that France officially surrendered to the Nazis and where immediately after the ceremony Hitler danced his curious, stiff jig for the newsreel cameras. There is no plaque commemorating this occasion.

121

PIERREFONDS

East of the Compiègne Forest stands the fantastic Château of Pierrefonds with its crenelated gates, soaring towers, and conical spires. Perched high on a promontory above the town, it suggests Ludwig's Bavaria more than it does 19th-century France, the period when it was reconstructed by Viollet-le-Duc, some 300 years after Louis XIII tore down the original feudal pile.

123

Chartres Cathedral: Rodin Called This Gothic Masterpiece the Acropolis of France

Several earlier shrines stood here before a great surge of religious fervor raised this cathedral in the late 12th and early 13th centuries. The preceding church, ravaged by fire in 1194, con-

Chenonceaux Bridges the Cher; Royal Ladies Laid Out Its Flaglike Gardens

The four-century-old chateau flourished under two famous hostesses: Diane de Poitiers, mistress of Henry II, and Catherine de Médicis, Henry's widow, who evicted Diane. Louise of Lorraine, the "White Queen," retired to mourn here when Henry III died.

tributed the main façade and the two towers, now topped by totally dissimilar spires—Romanesque (left) and Gothic. Some 4,000 statues embellish the exterior. The 174 stained-glass windows include several roses; one shows here above the south transept's triple doors. Crowded houses block an over-all view from the ground; the author made this picture from a helicopter.

Church and Statue Cap Volcanic Plugs Overhanging Le Puy

An ancient center of the lacemaking industry, Le Puy means "the Peak" in the Auvergne dialect.

St. Michel's Chapel, ten centuries old, crowns the volcanic exclamation point at left. Visitors to the 280-foot summit climb 267 laborious steps. Residents call this spectacular outcropping Aiguilhe (the Needle) because of its prominence.

Corneille Rock (center) bears a lofty Madonna and Child cast from 213 Russian guns captured during the Crimean War.

During the Middle Ages, great pilgrimage crowds flocked to the Cathedral of Notre Dame du Puy (right) to venerate a Black Virgin reputedly taken from Egypt by Louis IX.

daughters in a two-horsepower Citroën—the humblest, homeliest, most popular car in France.

"A superb car!" a Paris taxi driver once described it to me. "It goes anywhere, costs almost nothing to run, and never gives any trouble. It's like a homely wife who's a good cook and very agreeable to live with."

Le Puy had changed little since our 1950 visit.* The strange old cathedral, with its multicolored Moorish masonry, the bronze Virgin on Corneille Rock, and the chapel of St. Michel standing atop a volcanic pinnacle still drew thousands of pilgrims.

The near-by feudal fortress of Polignac still guarded its brood of red-roofed houses. In the warmth of an idyllic afternoon, the tidy, open fields teemed with activity. Oxcarts creaked and rumbled. A sturdy woman

and a little boy sowed barley and plowed it under with two white cows. An old woman washed sheets in an outdoor laundry. An attractive miss sat watching her cows, crochet needles dancing in her busy fingers. Her shaggy shepherd dog trotted around importantly, and a pet goat tried to eat her skirt. No, things had not changed here since our last visit; perhaps not for centuries.

Fields That Feed Half of France

But French agriculture is not all primitive. It is actually more productive, acre for acre, than our own, although it takes five Frenchmen to feed ten, while one American farmer does the same job. The fertile plains between Flanders and the lower Loire, worked

* Charms of the Le Puy region are described in "France's Past Lives in Languedoc," July, 1951.

738

CHARTRES

(Left) Generally regarded as France's most beautiful cathedral, Chartres is a masterpiece of early medieval architecture. It soars from a little village elevated above the flat wheatfields of La Beauce fifty-five miles southwest of Paris. The towers were built in different periods: the one on the right, dating back to 1165, is Romanesque-Lombardic; the left tower, rebuilt in Gothic style in 1506, replaced its predecessor which was destroyed by fire.

The 12th- and 13th-century windows, jeweled in brilliant bursts of blue, red, green and brown, are considered the finest in the world, and the statues flanking the outside porches, with their sensitively carved faces, are supreme examples of French sculpture.

AMIENS

(Below) Eighty miles northwest of Paris, in Picardy, the enormous Cathedral of Amiens (France's second largest after Rheims) rises above this city of 100,000 people. The town of Amiens was virtually leveled in both World Wars, but the cathedral escaped serious harm and now has had much of its 13th-century splendor restored. The intricate reliefs of the façades depict ancient fables, mystery plays and moralities as well as those crafts once practiced by Amiens' artisans. The choir's woodwork is considered the world's finest. Both Ruskin and Proust have written about it at some length. The steeple and fine rose window were added in the 16th century.

ORLEANS

(Above) Detail of the transept of the Orléans Cathedral, and home of Joan of Arc, saviour of the city.

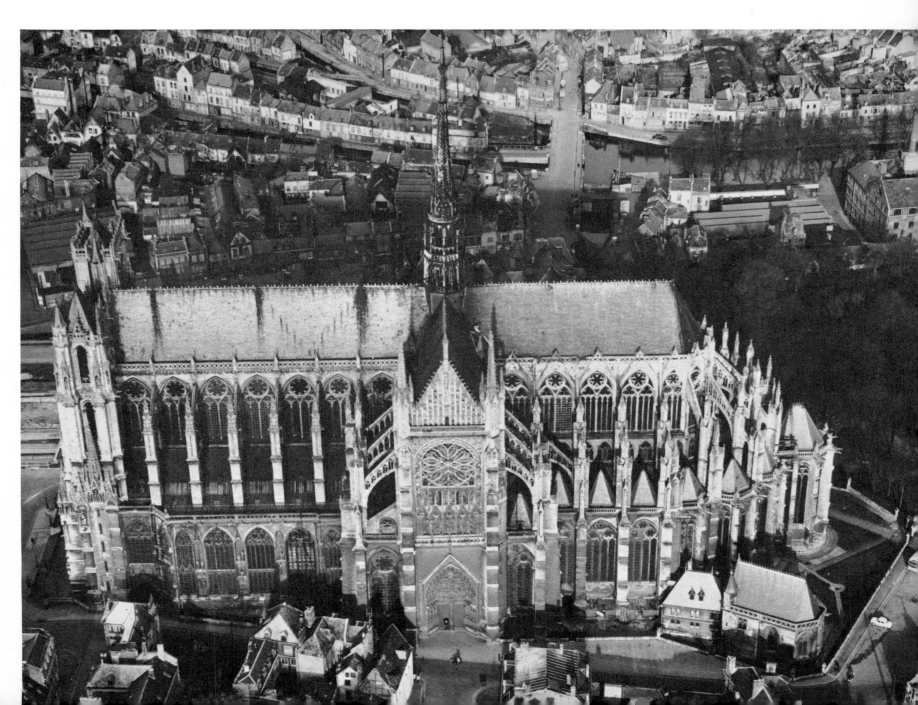

VALLEY OF THE LOIRE

The Loire River, with many tributaries, from its headwaters just west of Lyons to the ship-building town of St. Nazaire, has been a busy waterway from early Roman times to the present. From the region's lush hillsides, fertile valleys, and rich plains come the plums of Tours, the pears of Anjou, Vendome's cheeses and the magnificent wines of Vouvray, Coteaux du Layon, and Pouilly-sur-Loire.

It is little wonder that, for half a millennium now, both noble and commoner have settled here to build the lovely towns, thriving cities, handsome churches and manors. No matter what the inhabitants' background, they made the most of this bountiful area.

The gentle Loire rises in the Ardèche region and flows north, in a great arc, past Roanne, Nevers and Orléans, before turning westward to Blois, Tours, Angers and Nantes. Near its banks stand some of France's most historic structures: the great Château of Chambord, the castle at Angers and the cathedral at Tours.

(*Above*) 120 miles south of Paris is the old town of Sancerre, its houses clustered at the base of the Château. Its Tour des Fiefs commands an extensive view of the Loire Valley.

(Above) A village on the Loire near Nevers. The houses form an almost continuous façade the full length of the main street down to the river. In all likelihood many of the owners have sizable farms in long narrow strips outside the town.

(Left) A small farm on the south bank of the Loire, near Blois. The walled compound back of the farm is typical of this locality.

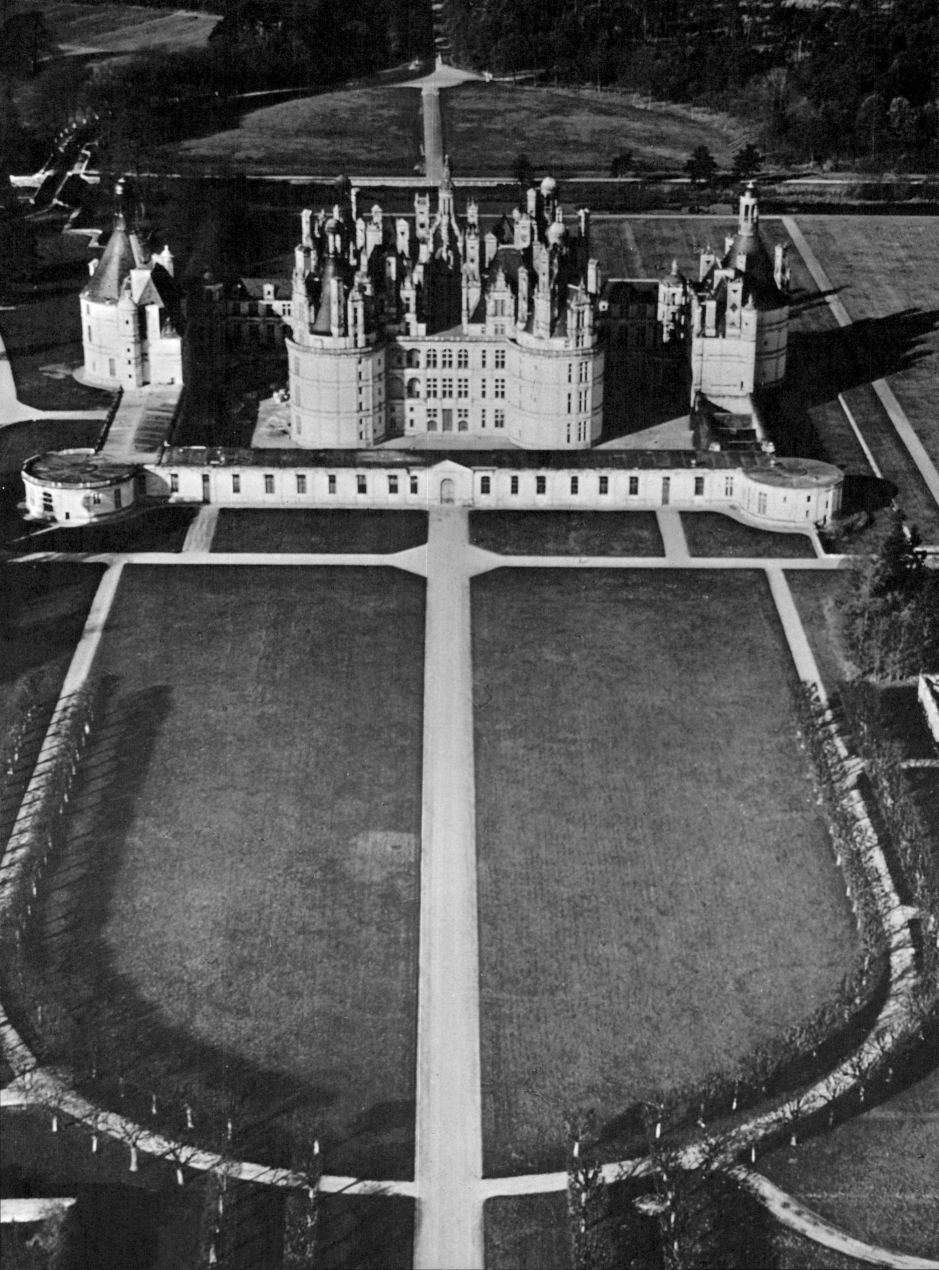

CHAMBORD

If not so beautiful as Chenonceaux or so dramatic as Blois or Amboise, Chambord is certainly the Loire Valley's largest château: it has 440 rooms and covers 200,000 square feet. François I built it as combined palace and hunting lodge. The central staircase is an architectural tour de force: two ascending spirals, like two interlocked corkscrews, pass each other but never meet. Another spiral soars a hundred feet higher, and from this height you can see the fantastic ensemble, a scene lifted from *La Princesse de Clèves*.

129

MONT-SAINT-MICHEL

Even had it been only recently built, Mont-Saint-Michel would be considered an overwhelming feat of construction. It was staunchly undertaken by Aubert, Bishop of Avranches in 709, when he built a small chapel on the island jutting out from the Norman shore into a tidal flatland of 100,000 acres.

The present Abbey perches on a granite hill 260 feet above those flats, which have unseen patches of quicksand; and for centuries it was difficult, and dangerous, to reach the Abbey from the mainland. An in-rushing flood-tide, or quicksand, could engulf the pilgrim. A causeway was erected in the 19th century, completing a ten-century project to lift Saint Michael's raised sword 500 triumphant feet above sea level.

As an object of pilgrimages, the Abbey was granted British immunity from capture during the Hundred Years' War, and French pilgrims were allowed to make their yearly trip to the Shrine. Over the centuries, its furnishings became more lavish, the Abbey grew rich and, inevitably, fell into decline. The main sections were finished between the 11th and the 16th centuries, and Bishop Aubert's Chapel was replaced by La Merveille, now the main monastery. What created the Abbey, spiritually as well as architecturally, was the masculine driving force behind the first Crusades.

The entire Abbey is surrounded by a fortified town and is entered by three medieval gates which are still standing, the Porte de l'Avancée, the Porte du Boulevard, and the Porte du Logis du Roi. Today, the small town is devoted to one industry: tourists. But the Abbey proper maintains its spiritual life.

131

LYONS

The third largest city in France, astride the Saône and the Rhône Rivers, and the home of Rabelais for at least two years, Lyons is now manifestly modern, having a heavy concentration of industry and commerce, even though in Roman times it had a far greater population. It also enjoys the reputation of a very excellent cuisine.

(*Above*) The Place Bellecour, with its equestrian statue of Louis XIV, is bordered with elegant 18th-century houses. Upper right is the Place Antonin Poncet and tower of the Eglise de la Charité.

132

VIENNE

(Above) This very ancient Gallo-Roman city lies sixteen miles south of Lyons. Nearby is the superbly preserved Roman theater, the largest in ancient Gaul, seating 13,000 people. Here, too, is Madame Point's Restaurant de la Pyramide, ranked among the great restaurants of the world. The gourmet must, and of course will, go to the Pyramide with plenty of time to spare, an enormous appetite, and the correct number of francs.

LYONS

(Left) The Basilica of Nôtre-Dame-de-Fourvière, which can be reached by a funicular railway from the city below. The 262-foot metal tower beyond was designed by Eiffel and built in 1893. The Saône River flows through the valley below.

133

MARSEILLES

The history of France's second city goes back 2500 years. Settled by Greeks from Asia Minor in the 6th century B.C., Marseilles has played an important role ever since. Caesar defeated Pompey here in 49 B.C., and, almost 1800 years later, five hundred volunteers set off toward Paris to support the Revolution, bringing a new warlike song: *"La Marseillaise."* Joseph Conrad was here as a young man, running guns for the Carlist Rebellion, as he tells in his autobiographical novel, *The Arrow of Gold.*

Warmed by the Mediterranean, Marseilles is one of the world's major seaports, where freighters from Africa unload their cargoes of fruits, hardwoods and minerals to return with the manufactured goods of Europe. Passenger liners ply east and west; fishing fleets bring in their daily exotic catches. Even sophisticated Parisians, those *gourmets extraordinaires,* reluctantly admit that the bouillabaisse served in the waterfront restaurants of the Old Port is in a class by itself.

Also, Marseilles is the site for Le Corbusier's revolutionary apartment developments and, less happily, for that architectural nightmare, the 19th-century Basilica of Nôtre-Dame-de-la-Garde which towers on its hilltop over the Old Port. Too, Marseilles has broad avenues and gigantic cafés. And of course there is the thronged Cannebière, one of the famous boulevards of Europe. But Marseilles's Old Port is the city's real core and character, the heart of southern France and the bridge to Algeria.

Where gladiators battled, bullfighters stride in proud parade before aficionados at Arles, France.

2,500-MILE CRUISE ABOARD THE KETCH
YANKEE

Adventure—full ahead! Sou'wester protects Captain Johnson from rains on the three-month odyssey of *Yankee*, third Johnson ship to bear the name and the first built for inland travel.

NATIONAL GEOGRAPHIC MAP
BY JOHN P. WOOD AND ELIE SABBAN © N.G.S.

STATUTE MILES

Canals   Roads

Rhône dams   Elevations and soundings in feet

ENGLAND

LONDON

Southampton
The Solent
Cowes
Isle of Wight
Dover

English Channel

Cherbourg

Rennes

Nantes

La Rochelle

NORMANDY
Le Havre
Honfleur
Jumièges
Rouen
Les Andelys
Conflans Sainte Honorine

Boulogne sur Mer
Abbeville
Dieppe
Amiens
Arras
Lille
Mons

FRANCE

PARIS
Fontainebleau
Forêt de Fontainebleau
Seine
Oise

Canal de Bourgogne

Loire

Montluçon

Clermont-Ferrand

St. Etienne

Le Puy

Millau

Montpellier

Narbonne

North Sea

Zaandam
Noordzeekanaal (North Sea Canal)
Amsterdam
NETHERLANDS
Utrecht
The Hague
Rotterdam
Gouda
Arnhem
s Hertogenbosch
Zuidwillemsvaart (Zuidwillems Canal)
Helmond
Donk

ZEELAND
Walcheren
Veere
Vlissingen
Ostend
Bruges
Ghent

BELGIUM
Antwerpen
BRUSSELS
Waterloo
Mons
Namur
Val St. Lambert
Liège
Dinant
Givet
Charleville
Sedan

LIMBURG
Born
Maastricht

LUXEMBOURG
ARDENNES
Luxembourg

Osnabrück
Münster
Düsseldorf
Julianakanaal (Juliana Canal)
Cologne
Bonn
FEDERAL REPUBLIC OF GERMANY

Moselle

Reims
Verdun
Fort de Vaux
Canal de l'Est
Metz
St. Mihiel
Nancy
Canal de la Marne au Rhin
Saarbrück
Strasbou

Epinal
Fontenoy le Château
Corre
Conflandey
Mulhouse
Basel

Pouilly en Auxois Tunnel
La Lochère
Dijon
La Rèpe
Châteauneuf
Pernand-Vergelesses
St. Jean de Losne
Besançon
Bern
SWITZERLA

BURGUNDY
Chalon sur Saône
Mâcon
Saône
Lausanne

Rhône
Geneva
Sion
Great St. Bernard Tunnel
Aosta

Lyon
Grenoble
Rhône
Andance
Charmes
La Voulte
Valence
Pont St. Esprit
Bollène
Montfaucon
Châteauneuf du Pape
Avignon
Arles
Durance
START AND FINISH OF 2,500-MILE TRIP
Ile de la Camargue
Tunnel du Rove
Marseille
Ile d'If
Toulon
Mediterranean Sea
PROVENCE
Rivie

ALP
ITA

Where gladiators battled, bullfighters stride in proud parade before aficionados at Arles, France.

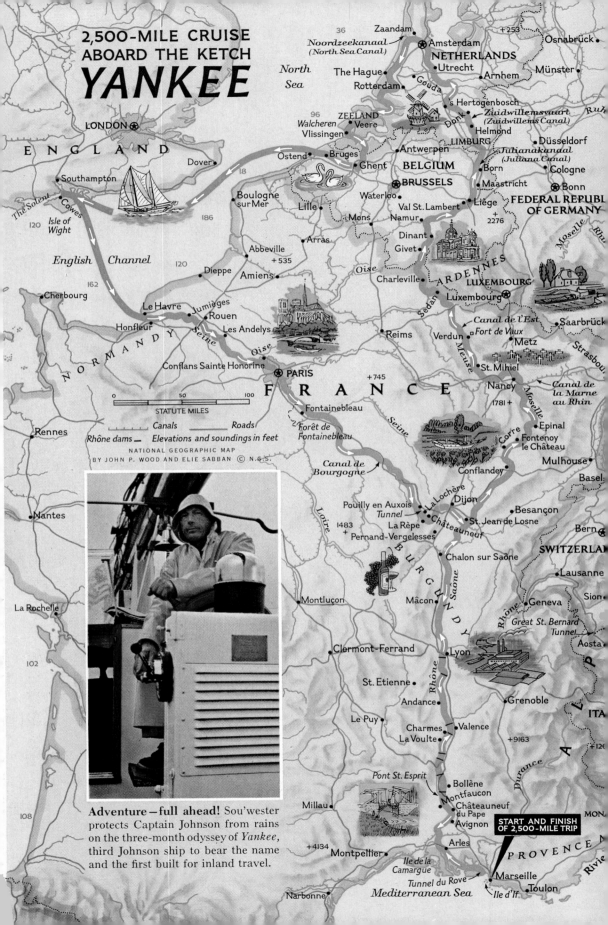

Adventure—full ahead! Sou'wester protects Captain Johnson from rains on the three-month odyssey of *Yankee*, third Johnson ship to bear the name and the first built for inland travel.

together in stormy friendship, discovered the strong light and color of Provence.

Greeks settled in Arles, but its greatest sights are the Roman ruins: a theater that seated 16,000, and an amphitheater for 26,000. Two tiers of 60 arches each form the arena's outer walls; today bullfights are held here (pages 164-5 and below).

At Arles we pointed *Yankee*'s bow up the Rhône toward Lyon, past ruined castles on the heights, remains of medieval town walls, and lush countryside. From glacial origins in the Swiss Alps, the Rhône gathers volume and power and races to the sea. New dams now are taming its lustiness, and on this trip *Yankee* could manage the currents under her own power. She carried us past Avignon with its stone bridge celebrated in song, and by such famed vineyards as those of Châteauneuf du Pape (page 168). But on our first trip up in 1960, we were glad to have a tow from a big oil-company barge.

166

(Right) On the hills overlooking the Vieux Port the 19th-century Nôtre-Dame-de-la-Garde is reached by a tunnel and a funicular that carries you to a high ramp and fine view.

The Old Ports. At the back of the harbor is the Quai des Belges, and leading into it from the left is the Cannebière, Marseilles' most important street. On the left is Fort St. Jean and the Quai du Port. Right: Fort St. Nicholas and the Quai de la Rive Neuve.

(Right) Rue de la République, one of the city's principal streets, runs down to the Quai des Belges on the waterfront.

(Below) This Arc de Triomphe, in the Place Jules Guesde, and west of the Old Port, was erected in 1833 to commemorate the wars of the Revolution and the First Empire.

135

COTE D'AZUR

(Left) Nice, founded in 30 B.C., is the largest most expensive city on the French Riviera, with its sun-drenched beach and hotel-lined Promenade des Anglais. Down this Promenade you will see, in what amount to astounding numbers, the world's most beautiful men and women, as well as the ugliest, in various stages of undress. Few of these splendid creatures are poor, which is as it should be in this clearly international playground.

(Above) Cannes, west of Nice, has one of the most beautiful harbors in the world. In the foreground is Cape Croisette with the Palm Beach Casino at its tip. The port itself, at the upper left, usually swarms with small boats, fishing vessels and elegant yachts. Ocean liners lie-to in the roadstead and passengers come ashore by small boat or lighter. Cannes' film festival, held once a year has to be seen, like Nice's Promenade des Anglais, to be believed. Beautiful or ugly, little matter which, nowhere else on earth will you see as many white teeth, blue diamonds, and brown midriffs.

ST. TROPEZ

(Above) This charming little fishing port
is one of the most fashionable resorts on
the Côte d'Azur. Its claim upon fashion
refers to nothing apparent, for the town
faces north, away from the Mediterranean's voluptuous breezes. Its popularity
refers, rather, to a number of stage,
screen and literary celebrities who have
unearthed "Saint Trop" and claimed it
for their own. The town has been important in the Mediterranean's long history
since the Greeks first used it as a fishing
port about 470 B.C. The Old Port is now
the setting for the annual May Bravade,
a three-day festival commemorating St.
Tropez. The Bravade evolves into a
rowdy brawl as Parisians, wealthy yacht
and villa owners, ordinary townspeople
and fishermen become progressively
drunker, progressively more amorous,
and more violent, until the festival ends
and peace descends—till next year.

AIX-EN-PROVENCE

(Right) The capital of old Provence, this
city, twenty miles north of Marseilles, was
virtually rebuilt during the 17th and 18th
centuries. Paul Cézanne had his studio in
Aix; ever since, it has been a favorite
place for painters. In the center is the
City Hall and, above, the Cathedral of
St. Sauveur, whose architecture bridges
eleven centuries, from the 5th to the 16th.

MONT BLANC

Astride the French-Italian border, Mont Blanc's cap of snow crowns the Alps at 14,000 feet. On the opposite side *(north)* is the winter resort of Chamounix, better known for its fashionable ski-center than for its herds of wild deer that range the mountains on every side. To the right is the Little Saint Bernard Pass, whose 7,500-foot summit Napoleon's army crossed, probably with Hannibal well in mind, in a daring maneuver in 1800. On the Swiss side of the Little Saint Bernard is the famous Hospice of St. Bernard of Menthon, an abbey of the Order of St. Bernard where, if only to sustain one of the world's best-loved traditions, the Alpine rescue dogs are trained.

MONACO

MINUSCULE MONACO—the entire country is one sixtieth the size of Paris and all of it could fit comfortably, if the shape were changed, into New York's Central Park—is wedged between France and Italy on the Riviera. What it lacks in size, "Montey" more than makes up for in celebrity. Officially, it is an independent principality, and it consists of three towns: Monte Carlo, site of the Casino itself; La Condamine, the port; and Monaco, its seat of government, perched on the sea's edge behind Fort Antoine.

While Monaco preserves the myth of independence, it is administered in practice by the French Government, which controls its borders and appoints a Minister of State who acts as Prime Minister. The House of Grimaldi, the ruling family, can, and does, trace its ancestry back to the 12th century.

Monaco is self-supporting, the bulk of the governmental revenues coming from the Casino. Its own citizens pay no personal income tax and are not allowed to gamble in the Casino. Moral?

(Below) Looking westward over Fort Antoine towards the Royal Palace and the coast of France. The Quai Antoine is lined with new apartments and the docks are teeming with small boats, fishing vessels and fancy yachts.

MONACO

From the sea almost the entire principality can be seen except for a small section to the left.

In the foreground, at the extreme tip, is Fort Antoine. The large white building is the Oceanographic Museum, which has gained considerable stature as a research institute devoted to marine studies. Reaching down to the sea, the hanging gardens of St. Martin's are filled with exotic vegetation. Just above the cliff and to the right of the point where the sea cuts into the coastline, stands the cathedral, and to its left, the Palace of Prince Rainier.

Behind is the port area of La Condamine and to the right is the Casino. Stretching up the mountain, Mont Agel, the splendid Moyenne Corniche leads, eventually, to Menton and on into Italy.

142

THE CASINO

(*Above*) Until Prince Rainier's marriage to the actress Grace Kelly, the Casino was easily Monte Carlo's most popular attraction and, for most of us, still is. It was designed, in Renaissance style, by Garnier, the architect of the Paris Opera House, and erected in 1878. At the right is a handsome terrace facing east toward the Italian border. The large round platform is used for trap-shooting.

PALACE OF THE PRINCE

(*Left*) The oldest portions of the Palace of Prince Rainier di Grimaldi go back to the 13th century, though the Palace has been added to and rebuilt several times, principally in the late Renaissance. The five crenelated towers of the original structure can still be seen. The royal gardens are to the left of the palace. Below: La Condamine with its boat mooring and public swimming pool.

BEAUSOLEIL

Europe's booming post-war economy has had its repercussions on little Monaco. With devastating simplicity, the country was once almost wholly devoted to the amusement of the very rich, those wealthy enough to afford villas and, at the spin of the Casino's wheels, to lose the equivalent of their sales prices. But now the growing prosperity of the Italian and French from the industrial north has resulted in a demand for small apartments and modest hotels. Builders have sought out every possible site that could afford sunshine and a view of the sea within rising confined terraces of brick and glass. This area, Beausoleil, is situated above and just east of the older part of Monte Carlo, and indeed some of it lies well within the French border.

GERMANY

Allied fire bombings, during World War II, leveled most of the old Hanseatic city of Hamburg; since then much of it has been rebuilt. Originally it was a bishopric and was chartered as an incorporated city in 1189. Today it is the largest "city-state" of the Federal Republic (West Germany).

Hamburgers make much of the lovely artificial lakes bordering their city. This one is the Binner-Alster (inner lake), the Aussen-Alster (outer lake) being beyond the bridge at the right. On the left is the Alster Pavilion, a well-known lakeside coffee house and restaurant, and alongside is the quay from which excursion steamers leave.

The street fronting the lake is the Jungfernsteig which, turning and becoming the Neuer Jungfernsteig, passes the elegant Vierjahreszeiter Hotel (Four Seasons Hotel). The street veering off at the left is Collonaden Strasse, which leads to the Botanical Garden and the University.

HAMBURG

Nearly a score of years after the first bombings of World War II, Hamburg still shows appalling signs of devastation. The gutted tower *(left center)* of the St. Nicholas Church will be converted into a memorial. On the right is the ancient Town Hall (Rathaus), which also houses the Stock Exchange. The bridges in the foreground cross one of the tributary canals of the Elbe River *(upper left)* which, as Hamburg's port and shipbuilding center, is bordered by warehouses *(foreground)*.

Hamburg, one of the greatest "free cities" of medieval Europe, has an old maritime tradition. A treaty signed in 1230 between Hamburg and Lübeck was the formal beginning of the Hanseatic League, the mercantile confederation which, expanding until it controlled the north-European export trade, attained enormous political power.

Hamburg played an influential role in the struggles within the Hansa itself; violent disagreements arose and led to the secession of member cities, one negative factor in the League's centuries-long decline. Another factor was the growing tendency of individual countries to protect their own merchants and withdraw concessions formerly made to foreign traders. Thus, in the 19th century the remaining Hansa property was sold, and the last three members, Bremen, Lübeck and Hamburg, entered the North German Confederation.

As all music-lovers know, Hamburg is the birthplace of Brahms.

149

UPPER RHINE

(Left) A Rhine barge moves toward the locks at the junction of the German, French and Swiss borders.

(Below) A small German village on the edge of the Rhine in the Swiss-German-French area.

AUSTRIA

VIENNA

(Below) The upper and lower Belvedere Palaces are separated by a long formal garden. The Upper Palace was badly damaged by World War II bombings, but has been restored. The Schwarzenberg Palace is to the left of the Lower Palace.

VIENNA

No European city better denotes imperial gaiety, pomp and circumstance, stately balls and courtly waltzes than Vienna—Vienna's myth, largely dead. Nevertheless, the city *is* devoted to music, the arts, and the good life, with little apparent concern about the economic aspirations of its larger neighbors—Germany, Czechoslovakia, Yugoslavia, and Italy. Not that life in Austria is easy; it is anything but that, particularly since the last war. But the respect and love that the ordinary man-in-the-street has inherited for music, for Mozart, Gluck, Haydn and Beethoven (who lived in Vienna much of his life, as Brahms was to follow), is without parallel in any other country. Even the garish advent of the juke-box doesn't seem to have lessened Vienna's appetite for great music; she still manages to reject the patently mediocre, to resist that ultimate modern temptation, the *laissez-aller* of artistic vulgarity.

Next to music, Vienna's second love has, as object, her own Baroque architecture, in particular that of the Innere Stadt (Inner City), which reached its zenith around 1870 during the reign of the Hapsburgs.

The Rathaus (City Hall) *(center right)* was originally constructed in 1872, its central spire crowned by the copper statue of a knight. The Rathauskeller (restaurant) is in the basement.

Directly behind the Rathaus and separated by the pretty Rathaus Park, is the Burgtheater, better known as the "Burg," and it too dates back to the 1870's. On the left, is part of the University, the second oldest German-speaking University in the world (1365).

The main boulevard separating the Burg from the Rathaus is the Ringstrasse, certainly Vienna's most famous street and one of the world's loveliest boulevards. Beginning at the Danube Canal, it swings in a full arc two miles back to the Danube. Upper right: Hofburg Palace.

152

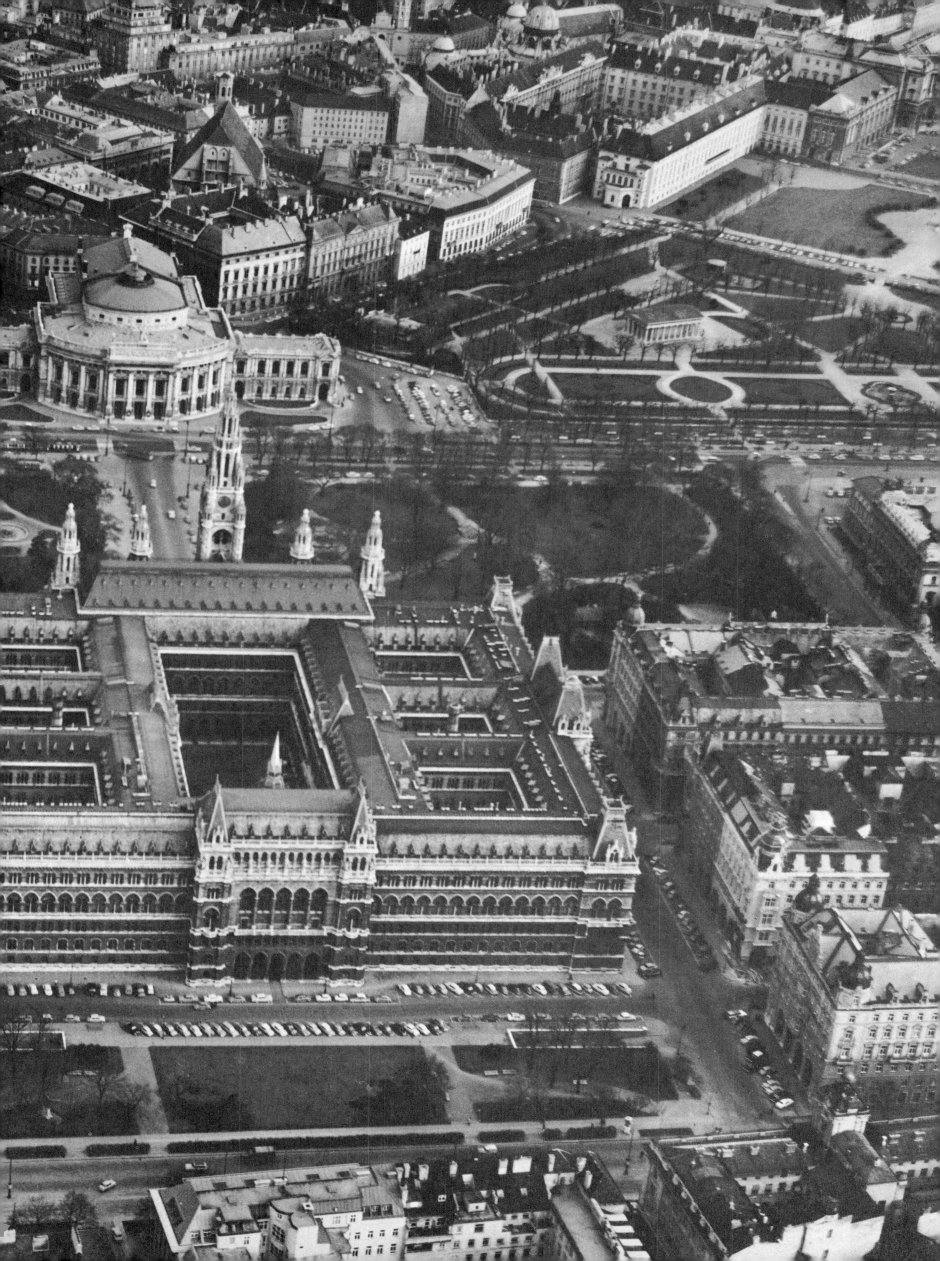

HOFBURG PALACE

(Left) The Imperial Palace of the Hapsburgs has been a Viennese landmark since its original construction in 1278. Essentially it is two palaces. The Alte Hofburg is the long building parallel to the large open area (Helden Platz) with its statue of Prince Eugen. The Neue Hofburg (with the arched colonnade) was built much later during the Baroque period.

KARLS KIRCHE

(Left) This Church, on the edge of the Karlsplatz was designed by Fischer von Erlach. Finished in 1739, it is flanked and dominated by two tall columns depicting the life of Saint Charles Borromeo, in much the same style as Trajan's Column in Rome. The City Museum is to the right, and the Ressel Park on the left.

SCHWARZENBERG PLATZ

(Above) The broad avenue coming up from the Schwarzenberg Palace meets the Ringstrasse *(upper left)* as it starts its swing back toward the Danube. On the Ringstrasse is the famous Vienna State Opera House (Staatsoper), one of the world's finest, which suffered heavy damage, as did so many buildings in the area, during the war. But it has since been restored to its former splendor. The fresh gilt and red plush of the interior provide an appropriate setting for the classic German and Italian operas produced there.

ST. STEPHEN'S CATHEDRAL

"Beloved Steffl," as the Viennese call their magnificent Gothic Cathedral of St. Stephen's, is literally that—beloved. When its 40,000-pound bell, *Pummerin,* originally cast in 1711 from a captured Turkish cannon, came crashing down in an explosion of sparks and flames because of wartime shelling, it took with it the Cathedral's superb tile roof and its 90-stop organ. All Vienna mourned.

But in a matter of days, reconstruction began—can Vienna be truly herself *without* St. Stephen's? Once again the cathedral spire, surmounting a double-headed eagle set in shining red and black tiles, reaches at the Austrian sky.

St. Stephen's started modestly as a parish church in the Inner Stadt in 1147 but burned down in 1276, into what are now the foundations of the Cathedral. Originally two tall towers were planned, and the south tower was built in 1433. Because of lack of funds the north tower could not be completed to match the other, and was simply roofed over with a cupola in 1506.

VOTIVE CHURCH

In comparison to St. Stephen's, this neo-Gothic church is modern and, many people consider, mediocre. Started in 1856 and finished in 1879 by the Archduke Maxmilian, it was built to commemorate his brother's (Franz Joseph's) escape from assassination.

157

SALZBURG

Even by European standards, Salzburg is old. The Celts apparently settled here about 500 B.C. Invading Romans converted the city to Christianity; and through the Dark Ages it developed into the northern bastion of Catholicism. The Benedictine Convent of Nonnberg, the oldest in the world, built there in 1000 A.D. and restored in the 15th century, is one of the town's many historic and artistic shrines.

In 1077, Archbishop Gebhard founded the fortress on the southeastern part of the Monchsberg, the great hill which dominates Salzburg on the west. The fortress withstood all sieges during those many wars that swept the area for centuries, and the strength of the German-speaking bishops grew until Salzburg was bitterly and justifiably referred to as the German Rome. When the Reformation came to northern Europe, it reached Salzburg so gradually that the city fiercely repelled her Protestants, and many of them were forced to flee. Ultimately many of their direct descendants emigrated to America, principally to central Pennsylvania. With the end of the Napoleonic Wars, Salzburg became an Austrian Duchy and, in 1850, was finally integrated into the Austrian Empire.

Salzburg's love of music naturally matches Vienna's, for it was Mozart's birthplace (1756) and home. Yet, despite this, it is more than ironic that Mozart's native city pointedly withheld proper recognition until long after his death. In 1925, the first annual International Festival of Music took place at Salzburg; and, though not wholly restricted to Mozart's music, the festival is now emphatically dominated by his image.

Today, Salzburg is a year-round tourist center, and one of the most charmingly situated towns in the world. Its picturesque squares and buildings border both sides of the Salzach River, which flows northwest between high wooded hills.

HOHENSALZBURG FORTRESS

(Right) On a mountain crag 430 feet above Salzburg, the famous Festung Hohensalzburg glistens in winter sun, over the haze-covered city below. Begun in 1077, it was enlarged with St. George's Chapel in 1501 and finally completed in 1681. Far below it on the right is the Erhard Church, built in 1689 by Caspar Zugalli, and to the left of that, on a spur of the Monchsberg is the Nonnberg Convent with its square tower and cloisters. Farther left is the tower of Kajetan Church and Hospital built in 1700. The center part of the old town is just to the north *(left)* of this picture. In the extreme upper right are the trees of the beginning of Franz Josef Park, the "Prater" of Salzburg.

SWITZERLAND

Insulated from the rest of Europe by the towering Alps, Switzerland has maintained her independence, and aloofness, from European quarrels for no less than 700 years, and has built a stable modern democracy which enjoys a high standard of living.

Because of an internal geography that keeps Switzerland physically divided, each of the three largest bordering countries—France, Germany, Italy—exerts a strong influence on Swiss culture and language. Hence in the Basel-Zurich region the predominating influence is Swiss-German; in Geneva-Lausanne, Swiss-French; in Bellinzona and Locarno, Swiss-Italian. But these differences are strictly nonpolitical, and each separate area, thoroughly Swiss, is and wants to remain bound to the Federal Republic. For leadership in both domestic and foreign policies *all* of Switzerland turns to Bern, the capital, never to neighboring states.

(Below) The Engadine Alps near St. Moritz. In the background the Bernina Glacier leads down from Piz Palü, a rugged mountain whose three peaks are nearly 12,000 feet high.

(Right) The highway down the south side of the St. Gotthard Pass to Airolo. Eighteen of the road's many switchbacks are visible in this short stretch: obviously the drive over a 6,000-foot pass is a tricky and exhausting experience but spectacular for the hardy driver. Most present-day traffic uses the railroad, which carries automobiles and passengers seven straight miles through a tunnel, thus shortening the one-hour drive to fifteen minutes.

RHINE VALLEY

(Left) In the upper Rhine Valley east of Basel, near the falls which Goethe described as "the sources of the ocean," stands this enchanting town with its double-spired church and sunny plaza.

(Right) This charming town, Rheinfelden, near the Rhine falls, crowds down to the very edge of the river. In the background is St. Martin's.

(Below) A country church and cemetery in the Rhine River's flat bottomland, east of the Rhine Falls.

BASEL

(Above) Basel is Switzerland's seaport because it is connected by the Rhine to the great Atlantic ports and northern Europe. The Rhine barges, some of them displacing up to 2,000 tons, ship an estimated 5,000,000 tons of cargo annually. As Switzerland's second city, Basel plays an important role in international banking and insurance. Culturally, the city was the home of Hans Holbein the Younger and Erasmus. Its Kunstmuseum, the finest in Switzerland, has an excellent collection that includes works by Holbein, Van Gogh, Gauguin, Rouault, and Mondrian, and many others.

ZURICH

(Right) Together with Basel, Zurich dominates the international banking world, and, like Basel, keeps the famous, and often infamous, numbered bank accounts of financiers and politicians from all over the world. These tycoons and near tycoons hope, in this way, to avoid their own countries' political disasters, income taxes, and currency devaluations.

But Zurich is a pleasant place, and much of its social and recreational activity centers around the lovely Zurich See. Sailboats are moored near the Uto Quai with its fine Theaterplatz *(left)*.

(Below) The Predeger Kirche and residential area along the Limmat River in Zurich.

Set on the edge of a sheer cliff, high in the St. Gotthard Pass near Airolo, this church and isolated village are typical of south central Switzerland's country near the Italian border.

GENEVA

In the eyes of the world, Geneva is *the* international city; it is the European headquarters of the United Nations, the International Red Cross, and the World Health Organization. On its streets you will see sari-clad Indian ladies, slit-skirted Chinese secretaries to legation officials, bowler-hatted diplomats from Whitehall, and correspondents from newspapers and press associations around the world.

Moreover, Geneva is a beautiful city. It borders on Lac Leman (Lake Geneva) and its French Renaissance architecture contrasts sharply with the Calvinist churches and those new banks and insurance offices. And, lastly, Geneva is rich. You will have to look hard, in this fortunate and immaculate city, to find a slum area.

It was in Geneva, "The Rome of Protestantism," that John Calvin settled and established his theocracy after the reform was successfully preached by the French humanists. Here, during the last twenty-five years of his life, he lived as an auto-crat-dictator making new laws and —as is sometimes the way of those who have successfully resisted persecution—burning at the stake his greatest opponent, Servetus.

In the 18th century Geneva became an intellectual center, and Jean-Jacques Rousseau, whose writings gave great impetus to the French Revolution, was born here. Voltaire also regarded Switzerland, or was forced to regard it, as his adopted country.

(Left) The Old Town is in the foreground, and the New Town across the Rhône River, flowing out of Lac Leman. In the left foreground rises the Mount of the Reformation; it contains a huge bas-relief dedicated to Calvinism and to the origins of the Reformed Church. On the left is part of the University.

(Upper right) The long bridge, Pont Mont Blanc, connects Quai Mont Blanc to the Place du Mont Blanc in the Old Town. Quai Mont Blanc is lined with fine hotels and steamer landings. Between the two bridges is the Ile de J. -J. Rousseau.

167

GENEVA, THE ILE

(Left) Connecting the old and new parts of the city, this Rhine island is straddled by the Pont de l'Ile. At the top is the Quai des Bergues and on the Old Town side *(bottom)* is the Quai Besancon.

GENEVA—OLD TOWN

(Right) The Old Town and the Cathedral of St. Peter. The cathedral was built from the 10th to the 13th centuries and was converted into a Protestant Church in 1536, after the Reformation. On its right is the Place-du-Bourg-de-Four, the heart of the students' quarters. The Rue de L'Hôtel de Ville is on the right.

LAUSANNE

This ancient cathedral town, thirty-eight miles east of Geneva on Lake Leman, was originally a 6th-century stronghold. The present cathedral was consecrated in 1275. Present-day Lausanne, both a center of commerce and a pleasure resort, has the Alps at its back and the pleasant shores of Ouchy, on the lake, at its base. *(Above)* The street at the right, the Avenue Benjamin Constant is the city's central business district. *(Left)* The Cathedral and the Old Town. Foreground: part of the University and the Place de la Riponne.

SPAIN

THE fifteen thousand bull-fight spectators packed into the Barcelona Plaza de Toros (below) on a warm Sunday afternoon, sum up many deep-rooted aspects of Spanish life. Out of the national temperament for grandeur, melancholy, and pride, the *corrida de toros,* with all its color, music, pageantry, rises from the arena's sand to a catharsis where man and beast, life and death, are equal.

Spain's known history begins with the Celtic invasions between 900 and 600 B.C. These were followed by Greek and Carthaginian influences, before those six centuries of Roman domination, when Latin gradually replaced the aboriginal tongue. Germanic invaders followed, and then the Moslems conquered all but a tiny portion of the peninsula.

By 1000 A.D. the splendor of Islamic Spain was at its height, and its capital, Cordova, was one of the most beautiful cities in all Europe. Many Christians became Moslem, but it was impossible for the two faiths to co-exist, and the long struggle for Christian reconquest began, ending in 1492, a date more familiar as marking a beginning.

The marriage of Isabella of Castile to Ferdinand of Aragon in 1469 coincided with Spain's achievement of unity as a nation and the beginning of her brilliant expansion as an empire. Spain was the most powerful country in Europe, until the defeat of the Armada by the English in 1588.

MADRID

In the middle of Spain on a high plateau bordered by the Guadarrama Mountains, Madrid was an undistinguished village until the 10th century. In the late 11th century Alphonso VI assumed control. He and successive rulers held the Parliament there, and in 1561 King Philip II established Madrid as capital of Spain.

Even though no king reigns there today, Spain still remains a monarchy and can (perhaps will) return to royal rule after the death or incapacity of the Chief of State (General Franco) by nomination of "the best-qualified person of royal blood," by the Council of the Kingdom. The Council consists of the President of the Cortes, the Cardinal-Primate, and the Commander-in-chief of the military forces.

Except for a very brief period, when it was moved to Valladolid, Spain's capital has remained Madrid. From here in 1808 the Spanish drove Napoleon's brother from the throne, the beginning of the end of French domination of Spain, and of Bonaparte's empire as well. Constitutional royal rule prevailed until the short-lived Spanish Republic was established in 1931. It fell, after the civil war of 1936-1939, when Spain's present government assumed control.

Modern Madrid is impressive and handsome. Skyscrapers tower over its ancient plazas. The crowded streets, as though a magician's wand had been passed over their entire length, become suddenly deserted about 1:00 P.M., for Madrid still observes the long siesta, often lasting four hours. The result is that social life begins late in the evening: the better restaurants do not even open their doors until 10:00 P.M., for the majority of customers won't arrive until midnight, and most theaters and cafés are crowded at 1:00.

(Left) The city's two tallest buildings, the Edificio Madrid and the Hotel Plaza, overlook the Plaza de España and Cervantes monument.

173

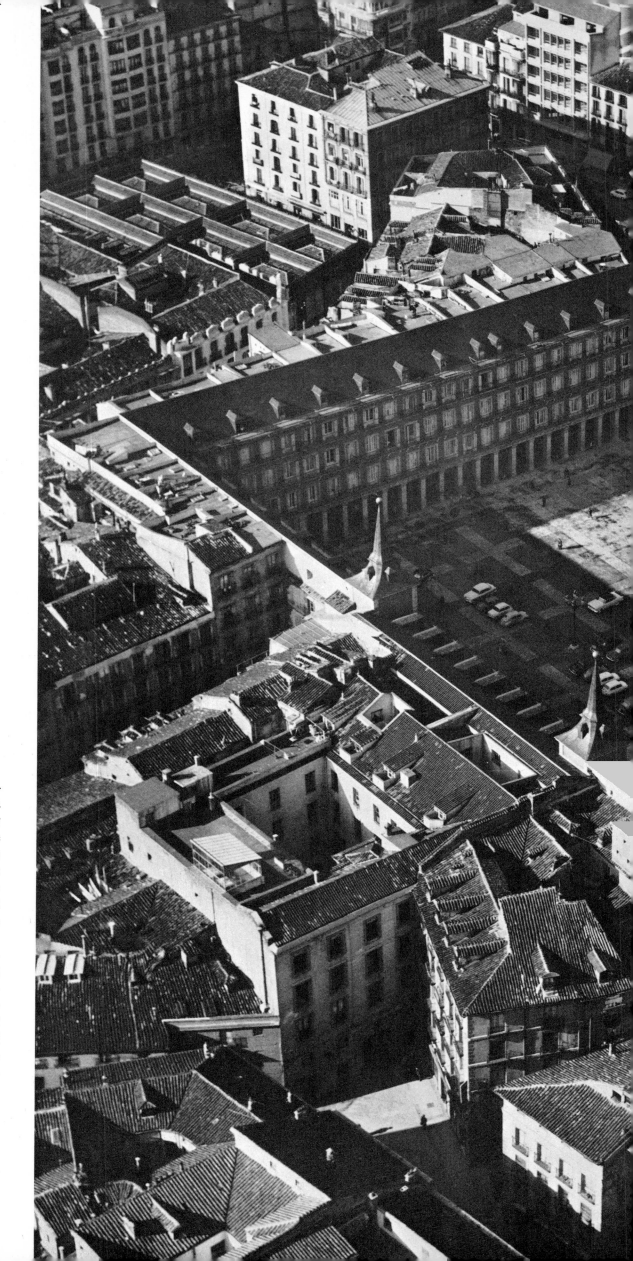

PLAZA MAYOR

One of the architectural master-pieces of old Madrid, the Plaza Mayor was completed in 1619 by Philip II. His statue stands in the center. The building with two towers on the north side *(left)* was begun in 1590 as the town bakery (Panaderia), but it burned in 1672 and was rebuilt to house some of the civic offices.

Much of old Madrid's lively public life centered in this square: bull fights, political and criminal executions, festivals, parades, tournaments, and open-air productions of Lope de Vega. The King himself used often to preside over these spectacles, from a balcony on the Panaderia. The arcades lead out to the Calle Mayor *(upper left),* and the Plaza de la Provincia and Calle de Atoche *(lower right).*

174

ROYAL PALACE

The immense Palacio Real stands on the hill once occupied by the Alcazar (town fortress) which was razed in 1734 by Philip V, who then sent to Italy for architects to rebuild it. And rebuild it they did, with a vengeance. Begun in 1738, the new building was completed twenty-six years later, at fantastic cost. The great square structure with its interior patio has several arcaded porticos in which stand statues of Roman emperors born in Spain, including Hadrian and Trajan, and one of Charles III of the 18th century, who attacked the Inquisition and did much to free Spain from her rigid medievalism. The large square is the Plaza de Armas, or parade ground for royal troops, and facing it, the Armeria or arms museum which contains a collection of old weapons and war memorabilia dating back to Charles V. Much of the collection, brought to Madrid in 1561, was pillaged and lost during the War of Independence, and later by a fire which also destroyed part of the Armeria itself.

In the foreground is the still uncompleted Cathedral of Nuestra Señora de la Almudena, the end wall of the nave and the windows lacking, but entrance is permitted.

The parterre garden *(photo, upper right and in the upper part of the Palace photo)* is Plaza de Oriente, with its statue of King Philip IV. Twenty statues of kings and queens surround the central plaza. Directly across from the plaza, stands the opera, formerly the Royal Theater, completed in 1850.

PLAZA INDEPENDENCIA

PLAZA COLON

PLAZA DE LA LEALTAD

EL PASEO

Madrid's elegant tree-lined paseos, on the city's east side, almost rank with Paris's Champs Elysées. Collectively referred to as the Paseo, the boulevard begins, on the city's south side, as the Paseo del Prado, and passes the Prado Museum and the Plaza de la Lealtad (Loyalty). This Plaza is dedicated to two officers who stood off the French on the 2nd of May, 1808, and their deed is inscribed on the obelisk there.

The Paseo del Prado ends at the Plaza de los Heroes del 10 de Agosto, with its lovely fountain of Cibeles, a statue of the goddess Cybele in a chariot drawn by two lions. Most Madrileños refer to it as the Plaza Cibeles. Continuing north, the boulevard becomes the Paseo de Calvo Sotelo, which ends at the Plaza Colon with its monument to Christopher Columbus. Then changing its name again, the boulevard becomes the Paseo de la Castellana as it sweeps northward to end, finally, as the Avenida Generalissimo.

On the left is the Plaza Independencia, at the end of the Alcala, and the entrance to the Retiro Park. This arch was built in 1778 to commemorate the entry of Charles III into Madrid. The patterns in both Plazas are made of grass and bedding plants meticulously cared for.

179

PRADO MUSEUM

(Above) The Museo Nacional de Pintura y Escultura, better known as the Prado, was founded in 1819 by Ferdinand VII and opened as a public gallery in 1828, the year of Goya's death. Its origins, however, go back to the private collections of many monarchs from the late 16th century onward. The Museum was later designed to gather under one roof many collections which had been stored or hung in various royal palaces and churches. Today, the Prado is renowned for its incomparable Velasquez, Goyas, Riberas, Murillos, El Grecos and Zurbarans. Along with the Spanish masters there is a superb assortment of works by Titian and Tintoretto and, coming down through the Spanish domination of the Netherlands, works by Van der Weyden, Jordaens and Rubens and the marvelous fantasies of Hieronymus Bosch. The whole collection is remarkably rich and varied.

Behind the Prado is one of Madrid's oldest churches, San Jeronimo, considerably rebuilt in the late 19th century.

PUERTA DEL SOL

(Right) This is Madrid's Times Square, its Piccadilly Circus, a crossroads into which seven major streets debouch. Madrileños come here on New Year's Eve to eat twelve grapes in time to the twelve magic strokes of the midnight bell. The Puerta del Sol's buildings are not old, except for the Public Security building (left center) which was built in 1768. The Puerta del Sol got its name from a painting of the sun over the gates to the old chapel of Buen Suceso, now replaced by the Hotel de Paris.

GAUDI TEMPLE

(Left) One of Barcelona's most singular characteristics is the incredible architecture of Antonio Gaudi, who died in 1936 and left behind him a group of unusual, not to say improbable, buildings; the most interesting is the uncompleted Temple of the Sagrada Familia (Holy Family). Barcelona is full of Gaudi. His churches, private homes and apartment houses have no straight lines, no sharp corners, and spurt alarming balconies and doorways in undulating waves of color, like open mouths with protruding lips. The flight of his wild imagination found startling expression in the Parque Güell, a children's park in the Montada Pelada district overlooking the city, a fantastic arrangement of pillars, stone trees, stone snakes, and monster-like fountains. The Holy Family church, begun in 1884, is his masterpiece. The four towers are 500 feet high. Construction goes on, in good part by popular subscription.

COSTA BRAVA

(Below) The Rugged Coast, or Costa Brava, is a magnificent 110-mile stretch along the Mediterranean from the French border to Barcelona. It is reminiscent of the California-Big Sur coastline as well as parts of the Italian Riviera. Early Phoenician, Greek and Roman traders first left their marks on these shores long before the birth of Christ. This village is Tossa del Mar, whose oldest part, behind its 11th-century crenelated walls, is called Vila Vella. The Costa Brava is particularly popular among French and English youths of both sexes, whose sports cars can be seen, any August day of any year, fish-tailing through the Coast's villages.

GREECE

AT THE TIME of the Siege of Troy, the early Greeks were well settled in the area of the Aegean, having absorbed the splendid Cretan culture they found established there, and had long since begun to develop their own customs and to colonize. Their city states and colonies prospered, and by the 5th century B.C., Greece was on the verge of her full flowering, one never since surpassed, if equaled, in the worlds of art and intellect. Science, philosophy, political thought, literature, architecture, and sculpture—all these are Greece's permanent legacy to the western world.

The heart of this civilization was Athens. The statesman Pericles, who died in 429 B.C., was a patron of the arts, and in his regime the Athenians, who spent little on their private dwellings, responded to his appeal for funds to rebuild the Acropolis. The result was the Doric Parthenon and those other supremely matchless buildings on Athens's hill.

Greece declined through the catastrophic Peloponnesian War, followed by the insatiable ambition of Alexander the Great, and then the power of Rome. Successive invasions through the following centuries by barbarous tribes of Europe reduced the land to a primitive state for hundreds of years, the remnants of culture and social life being preserved largely through the Orthodox Church.

In modern times, the 1821 uprising against Turkish hegemony established Greek independence, and the Greek state was created in a London conference in 1830, a convenient beginning for the complicated history of contemporary Greece. From 1821 to 1955, with the exception of a single thirty-year period, Greece has been in an almost constant state of warfare. The Greeks have fought Albanians, Yugoslavs, Bulgarians, Turks, and each other, as well as being hopelessly and devastatingly involved in both World Wars. The end of World War II brought Greece nothing more than a savage civil conflict lasting four long years.

For countries larger and richer than Greece such a history would have been damaging enough; for Greece, a small agricultural country of eight million people, it has been disastrous. Generations of Greek youth were killed; inflation split open her economy; her politics have been stormy, erratic and without foundation, changing from monarchy to democracy to dictatorship.

But Greece today offers a happier outlook, at least for the moment. There is peace within the country, economic depth, a stable drachma, and secure government, a constitutional monarchy. The ancient monuments have been made more accessible and thus tourism has become the country's third largest industry. By 1965, it is estimated, half a million foreigners will visit Greece every year. They will not be disappointed in this warm and friendly land.

THE ACROPOLIS

One of the world's supreme monuments, the Acropolis has stood above Athens from time immemorial. It served as a fortress about 3000 B.C. Later there was a large primitive temple to Athena in the approximate center of the hill, beside which, in the latter part of the 5th century B.C., Pericles planned and began construction of the Parthenon and the Temple of the Wingless Victory. In the 6th century A.D. the Parthenon became a Byzantine church; in 1209 the Crusaders used it for Catholic worship; and finally the Turks, using it for a powder magazine, watched it blown up in the Venetian War of 1687. *(Above)* The Acropolis from the southeast. The Theater of Dionysos is lower left, and the Theater of Herodes Atticus above it. *(Overleaf)* The Parthenon and the city of Athens.

THE ACROPOLIS

(Left) From the southwest, the Theater of Herodes Atticus, built in 161 A.D., can be seen in the foreground. It was recently restored and the great Greek tragedies are given here every summer. Above it *(left)*, are the Proplyaea (outer gates) and the Nike Athena Temple. Behind it and to the left of the Parthenon stands the Erechtheum containing the porch of the Caryatids.

CONSTITUTION SQUARE

(Below) Constitution Square, or Syndagma Square, is the center of present-day Athens. On the right is the Old Palace, which now houses the Greek Parliament, Council of State, and Ministry of Defense. In front of the palace: the Tomb of the Unknown Soldier. Around the square, on the left, stand many of the city's best hotels. *(Left)* Haghios Georgios Chapel perches on top of Mt. Lykabettos.

UNIVERSITY OF ATHENS

The University of Athens was founded in 1873, and is now made up of six faculties: law, medicine, philosophy, physical science, mathematics, and theology. *(Above)* The three buildings in the quadrangle are, from left to right, the National Library, the University Building and the Academy of Athens.

OMONIA SQUARE

(Right) Omonia Square, the busiest intersection in Athens, has a pretty mosaic design in its center, and multicolored fountains. Underneath is the subway station for trains to the Piraeus, the port of Athens.

(Right) This important modern boulevard is the Odos Patission, (Street of the 28th of October). The intersection is Aegyptou Square.

PIRAEUS

Themistocles, the hero of Salamis, having created the Athenian Navy, developed the Port of Piraeus, and the original design of long straight streets remains much as it was 2400 years ago. Because of the natural harbor and the city's dependence on the sea, whoever held the Piraeus controlled Athens.

In recent years the Piraeus has shared in the resurgence of the Greek merchant navy, which has risen to sixth place in world tonnage. The harbor is jammed with freight from every part of the world.

(Left) In the foreground is the Pacha Limani, the ancient port of Zea, which is now largely restricted to small boats and private yachts. A growing number of amateur sailors make use of this beautiful harbor every year.

The main harbor reaches off into the background and is used by ocean-going vessels and inter-island carriers. In the distant background the smoke of Athens's diverse industries mists across the harbor.

191

ROME

ITALY

IF GREECE created an ideal image of man's potential moral and intellectual stature, it was Italy which adapted the ideal to man's actual existence, and showed us the possibilities of living under spiritual order and temporal law, in harmony with the world of nature and the creative instinct for beauty. Like the many fountains of Papal Rome—which conveyed the purest mountain water, and still do, through superb sculpture of marble and bronze—the literature, the paintings, the architecture, the very way of life in Italy, continue to refresh and sustain us.

Italy's contribution is perhaps the greatest; her treasures of art are inexhaustible. Her remotest village may contain a chapel, a fresco, a street of surpassing beauty. Her landscape and skies are perfect, her people generous, courteous, and impassioned.

Many origins, many centuries of conflicting ethnic, racial, and religious factions have brought this about; and many foreign and domestic struggles and compromises. Before 2000 B.C., the Stone Age Ligurians lived there; they fought and intermingled with invading Etruscans from Asia Minor. Then Gauls came down from the north; the Greeks established colonies on the south and west coasts (a few towns in the instep of Basilicata are still predominantly Greek); the Latini came, from God-knows-where. And out of all this admixture ancient Rome began to take shape.

By 500 B.C., Rome had overthrown her kings and become a republic; and after the collapse of Alexander's empire in the east, Rome became not only the great dreaded power of ancient times but a civilization strong in purpose and law. Having conquered Greece, she adopted and imitated much of the best of Greek culture. She built imposing cities in northern Africa, southern France, and Spain. By 130 B.C. she was at the height of her power, and enormously rich. When the growing proletariat brought on civil war, Rome was ripe for the dictatorship of the Caesars, beginning about 60 B.C.

It is from this period on for several centuries that most of the confusing ruins of ancient Rome date. One needs a detailed guidebook and a sound knowledge of Roman history to really enjoy these astonishing and apparently helter-skelter remains of temples, forums, and arches.

One of the last great Emperors was Marcus Aurelius, a tolerant and thoughtful man. When he died in 180 A.D., Rome was still officially pagan but Christianity was well-rooted and developing fast. It was not until 313 that the Church received official recognition. This followed the conversion to Christianity of the Emperor Constantine.

Through the "dark" centuries of infiltration from the barbarous north, the Church somehow kept alive the essence of Mediterranean civilization, now modified by the Christian belief in charity and service. Civilization began to progress in isolated communities protected by feudal lords, which grew into relatively strong city-states often fighting ruthlessly with one another while, behind their bastions, they constructed gravely beautiful Romanesque churches and convents. Many men turned to the monastic life—and out of this spirit the first great artists, Duccio in Siena, Giotto in Florence and Padua, and Pisano, the sculptor, inaugurated the world's most stupendous age of great painting, architecture, and sculpture, which expanded in almost unbelievable richness, variety and skill until the end of the 16th century. It was fertilized and nourished by the repeated discoveries of Greek and Roman statues and manuscripts; it became a rebirth of serious thought and exploration in all fields of knowledge, and moved on into the countries of Europe to fashion the cultural and philosophical foundations for our modern world.

In the 19th century the various states of Italy and Sicily were united into virtually their present political form as a nation. The capital, Rome, is the most renowned city in the world. One finds here, and in the neighborhood, the art and artifacts of the Etruscans, a mysterious people whose written language has not yet been deciphered; the imposing ruins of ancient Rome at its zenith; the early Christian altars and catacombs; the splendid upsurge of Papal power; Renaissance palaces and their gardens; the Palladian, the Baroque, the Neo-Classic; and on up to some fine examples of modern civic and domestic architecture and art.

If less harmonious and graceful than Paris, Rome has a compelling gusto and grandeur. It sprawls vigorously and casually over many steep hills, so that one is almost constantly aware of its million rooftops, tawny-colored houses, and vast perspectives of both place and time.

ROME

The picture on the preceding two pages looks west from the north central part of old Rome, along the Via del Corso, and at the bottom center the Piazza Colonna. On the extreme left, the dome of the Pantheon with its open skylight; above it the Church of Sant' Agnese in Agone on the Piazza Navona. The Tiber curves past the Palace of Justice and St. Angelo's Castle. Beyond are St. Peter's and the long galleries of the Vatican. On the upper right, the Prati, a well-established and attractive residential district.

THE COLOSSEUM

(Right) The Colosseum's vast size is apparent in the photo opposite, dwarfing the Arch of Constantine to the left and the smaller Arch of Titus above. The imposing platform is the ruin of the Temple of Venus. Directly behind it, the Church of Santa Maria Nuova, and right of that, farther on, the Basilica of Constantine, a massive vaulted structure like a Piranesi engraving, where outdoor symphony concerts are given on summer nights.

PIAZZA D'ESEDRA

(Above) Near the central railway terminal, this plaza is adorned with two arc-shaped buildings containing many of Rome's finest shops, and with the modern Fountain of the Naiads, extravagantly aqueous, and an encouraging welcome to the traveler as he emerges from his journey.

THE TREVI FOUNTAIN

From the air this grandiose fountain of Neptune seems lost in its tiny square and nondescript neighborhood. Yet every foreigner comes here sooner or later to throw in a coin to ensure his return to Rome; little boys jump in to recover the offerings; dozens of tourists take photographs; young lovers loiter; vendors sell souvenirs; odd shops and restaurants are scattered around. It is all very real and very Italian.

196

TOMB OF AUGUSTUS

This circular mausoleum was built by Augustus in 28 B.C. to contain his remains and those of his family. It was later used as a fortress before being restored.

CASTEL SANT'ANGELO

(Below) In the pentagon-shaped park bordering the Tiber this curious structure was built by the Emperor Hadrian to be his tomb. Because of its underground connection with the Vatican it was later used as a hiding place for the Popes when danger threatened, and still later as a prison. Opera lovers the world over have seen La Tosca leap from its battlements.

THE LATERAN

(Above) The Basilica of San Giovanni in Laterano is the Cathedral of Rome and retains the same extra-territorial rights as the Vatican and Santa Maria Maggiore. The present nave is of the 17th century, clear in design but embellished with ornate details. The cloister garden, poetic and fragrant, is a cool retreat for weary sightseers. In the piazza behind the cathedral is the most ancient obelisk in Rome, near it the Lateran Palace and famous Scala Santa.

On St. John's Day, holiday crowds fire Roman candles at the thirteen huge statues atop the façade. A direct hit brings good luck.

SANTA MARIA MAGGIORE

(Below) A fall of snow one August day, in the 4th century, is said to have outlined the original plan of this famous and magnificent church, rebuilt at various periods, hence of incongruous elements externally but of noble proportions within, and featuring two very sumptuous, very sacred chapels. The campanile, Rome's highest, dates from 1277. One should visit this shrine again and again. It is generally considered the finest example of the classic basilica form.

VICTOR EMMANUEL MONUMENT AND PIAZZA VENEZIA

The great stone "Wedding Cake," which symbolizes the unification of Italy, overwhelms much of charm and interest around it, notably the Palazzo Venezia *(lower left),* now a museum of art and furnishings and an important library; and the Church of the Gesù, the principal Jesuit Church in Rome, built by Vignola in 1568 and considered the prototype of baroque churches.

THE BATHS OF CARACALLA

(Right) These great ruins are the remains of a building which contained pools to accommodate 1600 bathers. Built in 212 A.D., it had also shops, sideshows, gymnasiums, libraries, and galleries of art. It was used until the 6th century, and now serves as a summer theater.

PIAZZA NAVONA

(Left) This spacious and secluded square was formerly a center of fashionable life and retains somehow the sense of a more serene and dignified past, in spite of the swarms of children who play there. Three spectacular fountains adorn it, and two excellent outdoor restaurants make it a charming place to linger in on summer evenings.

PIAZZA COLONNA

(Right) Facing on the edge of Rome's principal north-south artery, the Via del Corso, the piazza is dominated by the column of Marcus Aurelius, built in 193. To the left, and designed by Bernini, is the Palazzo Montecitorio, now housing the Chamber of Deputies, on the Piazza Montecitorio.

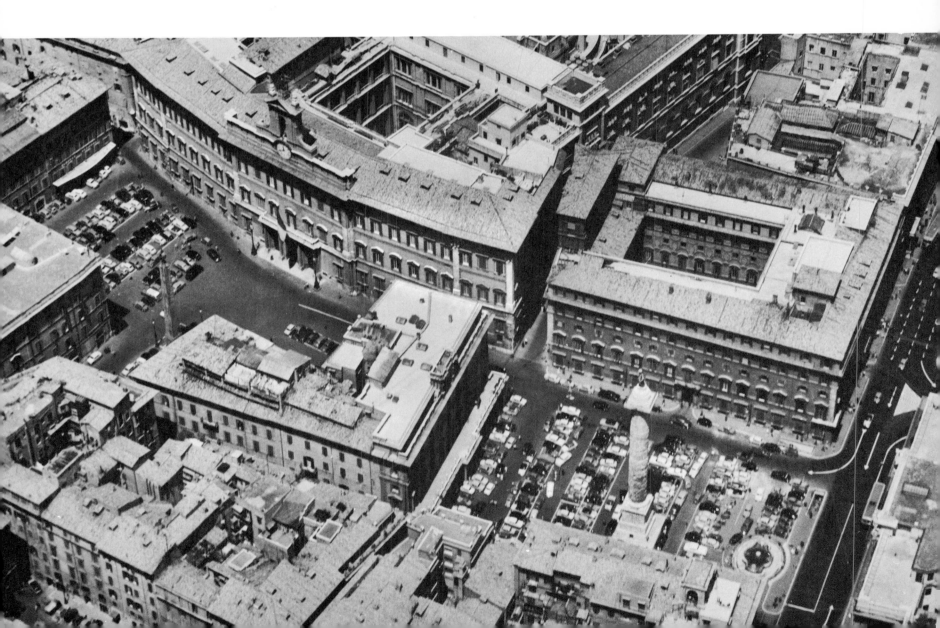

THE CAMPIDOGLIO AND ROMAN FORUM

(Left) The Piazza del Campidoglio, laid out by Michelangelo, covers a steep little hill, the Capitoline, in the center of Rome, and holds the Senatorial Palace (now the Town Hall) with its double flight of steps. Right, the Palazzo dei Conservatori (City Council) and, opposite, the Capitoline Museum.

(Below) Behind and downhill from the Campidoglio is the Forum Romanum reaching on to the Colosseum, and lined with the vestiges of old temples and market places. Upper left is the Theater of Marcellus, begun by Julius Caesar and finished by Augustus in 13 B.C.

TIBER RIVER

(Right) The Tiber flows through Rome from its sources high in the Apennines. The Bridge in the foreground is Ponte Umberto I leading to the Palace of Justice; and, above, Ponte Sant' Angelo with its statues of angels, and the Castel Sant' Angelo. In the background, the Via della Conciliazione leads directly to St. Peter's.

VATICAN CITY

THE VATICAN AND ST. PETER'S

The smallest country in the world, a third the size of Monaco, the Vatican is the spiritual center of the Roman Catholic world of well over 500 million people. Vatican City is completely autonomous, having been severed from Italy by the Lateran Treaty of 1929, which also gave the Vatican extra-territorial rights: three churches in Rome and the Pope's summer residence at Castel Gandolfo, south of Rome. The Vatican maintains its own postal system, and its own police and guard units.

The Basilica of St. Peter is unquestionably one of the world's wonders. It is incredibly huge—incredibly in the literal sense, because its scale deceives the eye. It was built on the Circus of Nero, where thousands of people were martyred.

The Emperor Constantine completed a structure here in 326 A.D. It was badly damaged by fire several times. Pope Nicholas V decided, in 1452, to build a new basilica. Pope Julius II commissioned the plans from Bramante in 1506 and work was started under the direction of Raphael and Michelangelo, who designed the massive dome. St. Peter's last architect, Maderno, designed the façade and completed the church in 1614.

The small building to the left, with the peaked roof, is the Sistine Chapel, noted for its ceiling frescoes by Michelangelo, and his altarpiece "The Last Judgment"; also for paintings by Raphael, Botticelli, Signorelli, Perugino, and others. This is the private chapel of the Pope, and the meeting place for the College of Cardinals. It is from the Sistine Chapel's small chimney that smoke rises to indicate the election of a new pope.

The Papal Palace and the Vatican are to the left of the Sistine Chapel and, in the foreground, the Casino Pio and its little paved garden, a gem of Italian landscape design.

205

ST. PETER'S SQUARE

The colonnade and the Piazza San Pietro were designed to accommodate half a million people. Giovanni Bernini, Rome's leading architect and sculptor in the 17th century, was still in his twenties when he received this vast building commission from Pope Urban VIII.

Bernini had several problems in designing so huge a public square. One was to give the entering pilgrim a feeling of being enclosed within the safety and confines of the church without, at the same time, being overwhelmed by massiveness. Accordingly, he designed the semi-circular columned arms which make the square seem considerably smaller than it actually is. Within those arms, he then designed the pavement with a slight slope so that every person standing in the square would have an unimpeded view of the Papal loggia, the balcony on which the Pope appears to bless the multitude.

Equally monumental is St. Peter's façade, designed so gracefully and in such perfect proportion that it is virtually impossible to grasp its true size (151 feet high and almost 400 feet wide). On top of the façade are statues of the Redeemer, St. John, and the Apostles, each of them eighteen feet high. Here too proportion holds; their size seems altogether average and quite normal.

206

VERONA

Relatively little known, except as a junction for trains going east and north, this is one of Italy's most beautiful and historic towns. Held in the arc of the olive-green Adige River are palaces, courtyards, civic squares and market squares of great age and interest. The Ponte Scaligero crosses over from beside the Castel Vecchio built (1353) by Can Grande II. Parallel to the river is the Corso Cavour, going northeast; near its far end the tower of the Palazzo Comunale. Most of Verona's churches are simple and austere, in the Lombard-Romanesque or earliest Gothic style. San Zeno Maggiore, of the 10th century, has a marvelous triptych altarpiece by Mantegna. Across the stream, beyond this picture, is the Villa Giusti, renowned for its great cypress trees.

(*Above*) Second only to Rome's Colosseum and seating 25,000 people, the arena is a perfectly preserved 1st century monument; it is used in summer for outdoor opera. The Town Hall (Palazzo Barbieri), shaped like a horseshoe, faces on the cedar shaded Piazza Bra. At the lower left is one of the gates of the old town.

PADUA

Three hundred miles north of Rome and twenty-two miles west of Venice, Padua was a center of commerce as far back as the 11th century. Its university, founded in 1222, is one of the earliest great centers of learning. Galileo taught there. Dante also worked in this institution, and knew Giotto, who was then creating the frescoes of the Arena Chapel. And Padua was the first city in Europe to found a botanical garden, which still exists, and appears in the upper center of this picture. It contains some remarkable exotic trees of great age. The fan-shaped plaza is the Prato della Valle with its islanded grove.

The church (upper left) is St. Antonio di Padova, dating from the year 1231, and, like most of Padua's basilicas, showing a marked Byzantine influence, because the town lay on the trade routes to Venice and the East.

(Right) Looking down on the eight domes of the Church of St. Antonio. An illusion, from the air, is that the two octagonal minarets, much higher than the domes, appear appreciably lower. Adjoining the church is the 14th-century Oratorio di San Giorgio.

VENICE

Even Dickens, who saw in the rest of Italy only relics of oppression and suffering, was spellbound by Venice, and wrote of it as eloquently as did Byron, Ruskin, Taine, Gautier, Howells, Molmenti, Yriarte, Corvo, James Morris, and many others. To the traveler who spends a few days there every part of it becomes an adventure as filled with wonder as is the tourist-thronged Piazza di San Marco and the trip on the Grand Canal.

This picture, looking southeast over the best-known part of the city, is so crowded with interest that one can only indicate landmarks. In Venice there are 450 bridges, 150 canals, and a labyrinth of narrow streets so entangled together that an air view shows little evidence of them.

(Upper left) Behind the Doge's Palace is the façade of The Church of San Zaccaria; to the right begins the Riva Schiavoni, the "sea-front" of the town. The campanile in the center (leaning ominously, like many of Venice's towers) is that of St. Stefano. A canal goes right under this church, with clearance at low tide. Near it the large end of the Fenice Theater; and below, the Campo St. Angelo. The long square running right from St. Stefano is the Campo Morosini, from which, past palaces and gardens, one crosses the iron bridge to the Accademia (its gable end visible), one of the great museums of Italy.

Along the Canal, this side, the big palace is the Rezzonico, very beautiful within, where Browning worked and died. Left of it is the Giustini Palace, where Wagner wrote part of *Tristan.* The palace with obelisks is the Balbi, where Napoleon stayed. Alongside it, the Rio Foscari leads down center to the Church of St. Pantaleone. *Extreme lower left* is the roof of the Scuola di San Rocco, known especially for its Tintorettos; then the apse and tower of the great church of the "Frari," austerely early Gothic but magnificent with tombs and paintings.

Near the Canal is the front of San Tomà (containing 10,000 holy relics). Beyond it and convenient for this charming part of town, is a landing of the *vaporetto,* Venice's waterway bus.

(Upper right) the Church of Santa Maria della Salute, and the islands of Giudecca and Giorgio Maggiore.

213

CANAL GRANDE

Still Venice's main commercial thoroughfare, nearly two miles long, the Canal is lined with palaces of many periods, some now hotels, a few converted to civic or business offices, and some privately owned or let out as apartments. *(Left)* The northern stretch, looking east from the famous Palazzo Vendramin *(lower left)* where Richard Wagner died in 1883, and which now houses, oddly enough, the Municipal Radio Station. At the turn is the Rialto Bridge; the twin white objects *(upper right)* are its roofed arcades.

Nearer and jutting into the Canal is the long Palace of Justice and the arcade of the Fish Market. Opposite, at the boat station, the celebrated Ca' d'Oro, a medieval palace once lived in (and nearly wrecked) by Taglioni the dancer, but now richly restored. The tower is that of SS. Apostoli, on the Via XXVIII Aprile, one of Venice's few long streets. In the extreme upper left corner appears the façade of San Zanipolo, one of the most superb churches of all, often known as Venice's Westminster Abbey.

(Above) At the eastern end of the Canal, is the baroque and coldly magnificent Santa Maria della Salute. At the very tip, the Customs Station, opened in 1682, is still functioning. West of the Church, especially on the water side, stretches the Dorsoduro, a favorite section for writers and artists, because of its simpler houses, gardens and relatively quiet atmosphere.

CAMPO S. POLO

About midway between the Frari and the Ponte di Rialto is this little-known, very typical Venetian square: old palaces, butcher shops, convents, tenements, *trattorie,* crowding happily together. In the 16th century it was a fashionable neighborhood; some houses still on the square belonged to distinguished families. The Palazzo Sorrano *(on the sunny side)* was built in the 14th century. For a time occasional bull-baitings were staged here, but were prohibited 150 years ago, for the Venetians are a gentle and animal-loving people—the city is thronged with well-fed cats, well-fed pigeons, and caged birds. And the lion emblem is everywhere, in thousands of stone carvings usually conveying a sense of affection as much as of pride. One palace on the Grand Canal has a whole row of lions' heads at the edge of the water, seeming to lap it, like so many kittens.

Campo St. Polo was also a favorite arena for factional brawls and free-for-alls. At the south door of its eponymous church *(with the tower),* Lorenzino de'Medici, a dwarfish and devilish specimen of the family, was murdered, in 1548, by his cousin Cosimo.

216

THE RIALTO BRIDGE

The Rialto is a sizable district, given over largely to finance and law. The courts, on the right side of the Canal, are crowded with activity. The Bridge, designed by Da Ponte, and planned to permit the passage of a fully-armed galley, was erected in 1592. Jewelry shops are under its arcades; vegetable and flower stalls dominate the center lane. People who want merely to cross or to gaze on the prospect, take the unobstructed outside walks.

This picture looks southwest at the sharp turn of the Canal. From the large square Post Office, mail carriers go out in boats to all parts of town. The Church of St. Bartolomeo, originally of the 9th century, and its lively little campo are just above. Here there is a statue of Goldoni, one of Venice's few eminent writers. *Upper left,* the Merceria, a fascinatingly varied shopping street, begins its somewhat wavering course to the Piazza of St. Mark's.

(Overleaf) ST. MARK'S AND THE DUCAL PALACE

Endless volumes of comment have not revealed all the details of historic, architectural, sculptural, and pictorial interest in this most famous group of buildings. Sooner or later every traveler finds himself, one fine evening, sipping an apéritif, in one of the outdoor cafés that line the great square, listening to the band play Bellini or Verdi, and marveling at the wonders about him. The next day, in all likelihood, he will explore the vast rooms of the Ducal Palace with their bewildering Tintorettos and Veroneses.

Suffice it to say that the Cathedral, for all its dazzling Kubla Khan exterior, is, within, a sombre place of devotion, and contains in its myriad mosaics some designs as simple and sincere as the art of Giotto; and that, along the waterfront, for all its tourists and pleasure craft, are still moored any day, cargo and fishing boats whose form and function have been unaltered for centuries.

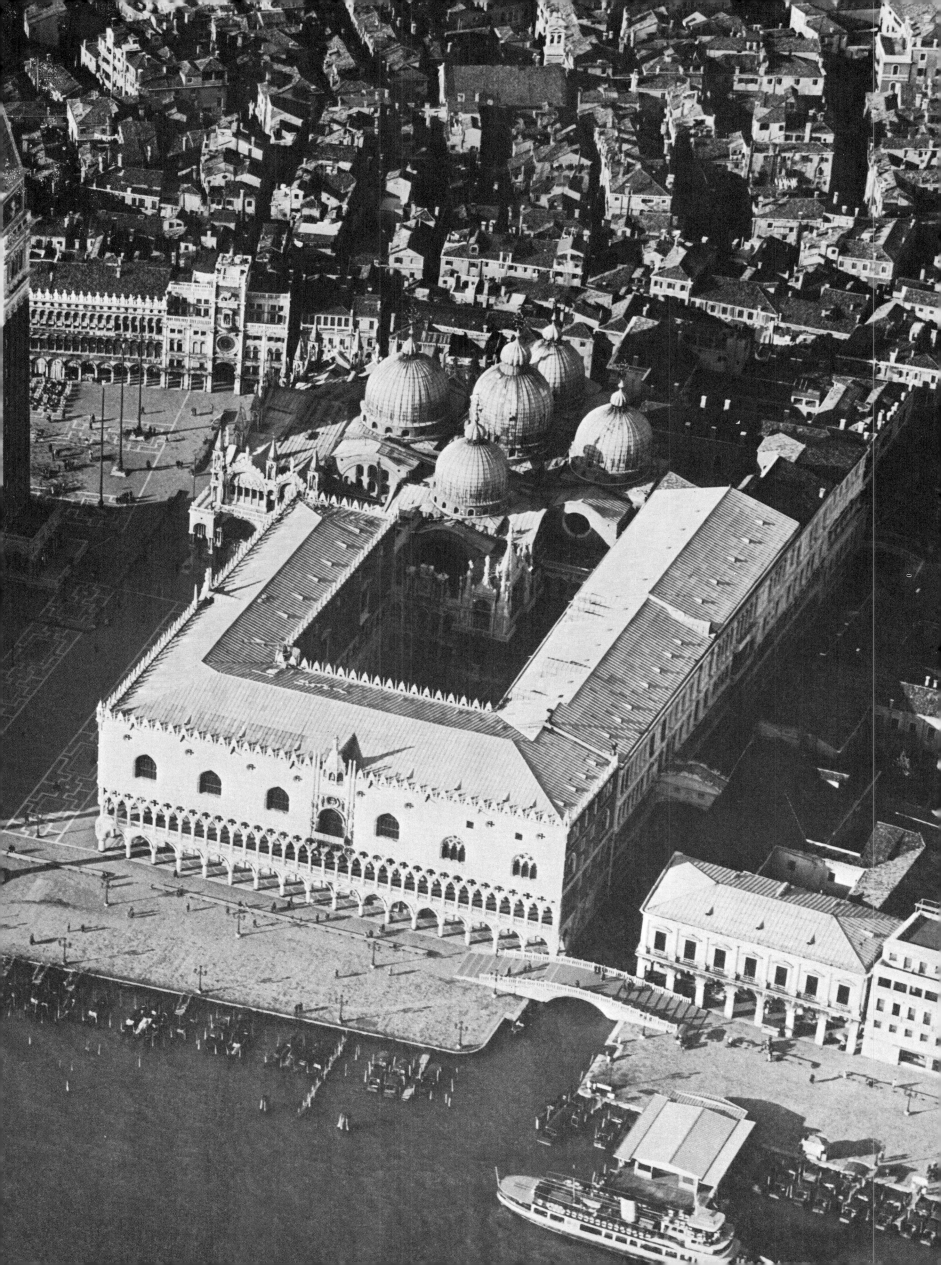